OPEN HO

OPEN HOUSE

with Katey and
Ross Lehman

Edited by Elizabeth Ball

With a Foreword by Sam Vaughan

Illustrated by Michael Chesworth

BINGHAM BOOKS

Grateful acknowledgments to the
Centre Daily Times of State College,
Pennsylvania, original publisher of
"Open House."

ISBN 0-9624756-0-2

Book designed by Irwin Wolf

*To Janny, Amy, Kassy, and Rob
and to Mary Jean and Frank Smeal*

A man's soul and life are his own,
and even if he gives himself away
in hundreds of careful and loving
pieces, he's still his own man
with his own life span, and no one
but he has a claim on it, except
his own God.

Katey Lehman

Foreword

THE local column is an undervalued institution. Local columnists are unsung heroes, nationally. Sometimes. The dean, the dapper don of them all, is Herb Caen, whose column is morning in San Francisco. He is voice, spirit, *Chronicler*, critic, and conscience of the Bay Area, and respected everywhere. Dave Barry started writing for a small newspaper outside Philadelphia and has since brought forth a syndicated column in 150 papers, a Pulitzer, and the latest best seller I've edited.*

Erma Bombeck began drafting ditties about diapers locally and was soon widely picked up, a national wifesaver. Art Buchwald was a curiosity in Paris for the *Herald Trib* before moving to Washington, where he has, ever since, made politicians quayle.

I've had the luck, through thirty-odd years in publishing, to know the best of them. Ross and Katey Lehman are among the best.

***Dave Barry Slept Here*, a mock history of the United States.

I say *are*, present tense, because Katey may be gone from sight but her spirit soars in these columns. Ross, gentle and heroic, is here in both sight and spirit, fortunately. Whether columns remain of local interest, usually intense, or circulate more widely in due course, the good ones have enduring value. Bruce Catton and other Civil War historians made excellent use of the letters, diaries, regimental histories, and newspapers in that writing-est of wars. Our future historians, biographers, sociologists, demographers, et al. will turn to the files of local newspapers and perhaps especially to their columnists, not so much for facts as for the feel of what people were like back then—and now.

When I graduated from Penn State in 1951, to take a desk at King Features Syndicate, a close friend and classmate of mine went to work for the Julius Mathews Special Agency, a first-rate newspaper advertising firm (now called Landon Associates). Their slogan was: "All news is local news." I've chewed on that phrase since, and in a way, of course, it is true. A bombing in Lebanon, a plane crash in Paris, a piano-contest winner in Moscow, all come home and cause us to hurt more, care more, if one of our own is involved. The fall of a leaf outside your window matters more than the firing of a forest in Sweden.

Some local writers are universal. They speak not only to the residents of a region but to all of us. Some tend to write less of the Rich & Famous and more of the meek, who are busy inheriting the earth, after taxes. Such a pair were the Lehmans, Secretaries of the Interior, in particular that environmentally endangered area around the heart. They were, among other worthy callings, curators of the customs of children and nature. Now, in this book, skillfully and sensitively edited by

Liz Ball, they are once again between the covers, together now for all time.

Were they unsung? Katey wrote, for both of them, that in contrast to the children in their lives:

> I have no song
> of my own to sing.

Ah, but they did—and do, here. Listen to them. How happy we can be that they and their work did not go unsung or unsinging.

Sam Vaughan
Senior Vice President
and Editor, Random House

Editor's Preface

W HEN Katey and Ross Lehman first put their heads together at Penn State in 1942, they expected their union to produce love, marriage, and baby carriages, certainly. And it did. It was likely also to encompass a journalistic endeavor or two, given that their first collaboration was on the college paper. This too came to pass. But they never dreamed that thirty-eight years later their conjunction would have produced seven-thousand-plus newspaper columns.

Invited as guest columnists, during the early years of their marriage, for A. R. Warnock's "Daily Half Colyum" and, later, for Lou Bell's "Once Over Lightly," the Lehmans earned the loyalty of a delighted *Centre Daily Times* readership. The local columnist's traditional blend of commentary, home-grown philosophy, and whimsy was just their brew, and in 1954, a few years after the family resettled in State College, "Open House" with Katey and Ross Lehman became a regular source of community refreshment. It appeared five days a week, fifty-two weeks a year, until 1980. Katey Lehman died on January 2, 1981.

Ross calls Katey the better writer. "The columns ran out on her paper like a clear stream. Me, I would sit down at the typewriter . . . and sweat. "Both of us felt peculiar about writing 'Open House,' even after years of it—a little uneasy, a little unsure. Katey wanted to quit occasionally. It gave her an eerie feeling to observe others as a stranger, as one apart, and to look upon them as beautiful, tragic, sad, mad, bad, glad individuals who suddenly appeared in a new light under the typewriter ribbon. Scanning people, following them in their daily pursuits, causes heartache as well as happiness. We looked upon futility and hope, death and life. And sometimes we'd like to have left things as they were, without comment."

But "Open House" never left things as they were; it put things in that new light, for better or worse. Katey and Ross's perspectives on life and love, marriage and child rearing, nature and philosophy, and—above all—people, gave their columns wide appeal and unforgettable flavor. They understood the universal human yearning to explain ourselves, to chronicle life as we find it. Each of us, Ross has said, writes a daily column in one way or another, for others to read. The Lehmans just put it down on paper in our behalf.

Most important, though, for more than twenty-six years they provided one little corner of the newspaper where readers could curl up and feel good, "a corner for sitting and thinking and rocking with their thoughts," as Katey put it, "so people will know, after they read the wicked news of the day, that there was someone who thought and wrote something warm and full of care."

The hard part was choosing just a few of the coziest corners to curl up in here.

Elizabeth Ball

Contents

Seasons

Prologue

THERE are times when the little people, the young people, the not-so-young people, and the old people, all of them, come into my life and leave me longing for them.

And all of them have different things to say to me. The little ones crawl up to my ear and whisper their shy secrets. Or they bounce on my back with too much vigor and more love than they can handle, and certainly more than I can handle graciously.

The very young but not so little burst into my heart and kitchen with what they consider "wonderful news, Mom," and it turns out to be nothing more than a Girl Scout cookie sale.

The young but nearly older, the tender ones who are part vulnerable and part strong, part day and part night, come to me with the fire of being and a need to care or be cared for.

The older young laugh with me in the intimate, knowing way that contemporaries have with each other.

And there is a soft poignance in the eyes and hands of those who are so much older than I.

I walked into a room holding a four-year-old hand in mine, and in the room I saw the mottled hands of a retired gentleman. They were busy, kindly hands, like those of my little four-year-old, but more purposeful, more sure, and even so, they were still touching, tenderly reaching toward life.

The young cheeks are dimpled. The old ones are dimply wrinkled. The young eyes sparkle like dewdrops. The old ones are distantly dewy, like the misty sparkle of faraway stars.

And all the voices, young and old, float up to my ear and whisper their gentle songs, wispily, singingly, secretly, lovingly, reachingly.

And so it is that I have no song of my own to sing, and no wee whisper of a secret to put somewhere into the gigantic ear of the universe. It listens, the universe, I suppose, and it longs, too, for the little people, the young, the not-so-young, and the very old. It must listen, it must see, if only because I, with no song of my own, have heard so much and longed so much to listen well.

—**katey**

REMEMBRANCE

When I was young 1

Ross is a reminiscent person. He's always harking back to "the days when," even though he enjoys the days now. The days now involve relationships with his parents that aren't too joyful, and problems with kids that are sometimes annoying, and problems with his wife and his psyche that are occasionally diverting.

Beside Ross's memories, mine are only shadows. I never got pushed out of a burning airplane, for example, when I was shot full of flak and someone had to keep yelling in my ear, "Pull the ripcord!" Ross wouldn't want me to get into such a situation. But I had a childhood, too, and I have memories, and maybe they aren't very exciting, but I can still smell them.

I can feel them, too. Some of them weren't very pleasant, and that's where I differ from Ross. I won't gloss over childhood memories of walking through fields of Queen Anne's lace and other hot, sticky weeds that scratched my bare legs.

I will not also gloss over the fact that after I had jumped joyously from a haymow into the hay for an entire afternoon in a generous someone's barn out near where I get apples now, I suffered untold tortures in the bathtub that night, from scratches I didn't know I was getting.

There's no torture in the world like the sting from jumped-on hay when the bath water crawls over an unthinking little body like mine was then.

Oh, but I have happy memories. Like Ross, I have good things to remember. I remember the way my mother canned the vegetables that my father grew in his garden, and I remember the gardens. And I remember the good things she cooked and the numerous people she fed.

No cook in the world was as good as my mother, and no gardener as good as my father.

I found the sky and the stars when I was a child, in addition to a recipe for meat loaf. I found lullabies and baked potatoes, the square knot and quilts. I found love and disagreements, roller skates and bumps, fudge and ice cream, and the Encyclopedia Britannica.

I found mountain laurel and ferns, brook trout, cold streams that made my feet ache, hearth fires, paths in the woods, Scotch scones with melting butter, cones from trees, clean sheets, and people who cared about living.

I also found a daddy who told me made-up stories and a mother who made me wash behind my knees.

In remembrance, one can skip a great many years. An individual can remember only the softly singing months or years, only the "one time" or the "one thing" or the "one year" from all that there is to remember, only the ones that made him glad, forgetting the ones that made him sad.

I remember the sad and the glad, and I would wish for all people that they recall the good that has come to them, and take from the bad that has come to them all the good that they can.

—**katey**

I T's peculiar how a song triggers a memory of an experience one had many years ago, and I recently heard such a song, "Blessed Be the Tie That Binds," that carried me back to my "saving" episode.

My father was a minister in a small town when my twin brother, Bruce, and I were about seven years old. We weren't bad kids by ordinary standards then, at least not by proverbial standards that labeled a minister's son as a potential or actual heller.

We were, of course, exposed more than usual to stimulants for being good and warnings about the devilish ways of Satan. Our two-or-three-times-a-Sunday subjection to our father's sermons and the continual references to the Scriptures made us aware that being good or bad depended upon God's surveillance of our daily lives.

One Sunday afternoon, a pal of ours came over to our parsonage and told us that a revival meeting was occurring in another church. Perhaps as a result of boredom at listening to our father Sunday after Sunday, as well as curiosity about what a revival meeting was, the three of us decided to attend.

We neglected, as kids do, to inform our parents where we were going. We took off like little sinners into a new experience.

The revival meeting was conducted by a visiting preacher who certainly proved to us that he knew how to save souls. He started his sermon by outlining the evils that existed in our lives and souls. He exhorted us about unthinking sins that we committed daily.

I thought of the flies' wings I had amputated, the braids I had stealthily sunk in my inkwell, the teasing of my sister Marian about her current boyfriend and his freckles, the last piece of pie I had stolen from my mother's pantry, the little white lie I had told my stern father, and the awful purloining of three ripe tomatoes from our neighbor's September garden.

As these sins filled my mind, they were accompanied by the rising voice of the preacher calling the fates of fire and brimstone upon us if we did not come to the altar to be saved. He pictured this terrible place with such color that we felt as if we were at the brim of the smoky pit.

In the background the congregation sang softly, and suddenly the preacher implored all of us to change our sinning ways. He pleaded with us to get up, move toward the altar, and confess our sins, while the music blended with his voice in harmonious supplication. There was only one thought, spontaneously, in our minds: get to that altar. And in a consorted movement, hands linked, the three of us marched up the aisle and knelt. We were saved.

The next day, the town was buzzing with the news that my father's sons had been saved by another preacher. He had beaten our father to the task of rescuing our souls. In the grocery store and the harness shop, men and women joked about "The Great Save."

My father? It's good he had a sense of humor. "Well," he commented as neighbors dug slyly at him, "one save is as good as another. After all, it's all in the family."

—ross

My new teen-ager asked me, "How many boys did you kiss when you were young?"

As I recall, I chuckled quietly for a minute, because I was trying to get it through my head that I wasn't "young" to her nor "old" to other people, and I wanted much to know whether I was young or old.

When I was young, what was the meaning of it?

When I was young, I kissed the bark of trees and let raindrops fall all over me, loving especially those that fell uniquely on my mouth or cheeks.

When I was young, I held a dying sparrow in the palm of my hand and grieved for him. When I was young, I climbed to the top of a cherry tree, cushioned myself in a branch, and ate the dark red cherries, spitting the seeds down there on the earth below.

When I was young, I investigated. I found a rabbit nest and held briefly a very little rabbit, and let it go. I found an insecure boy who liked trapping bees and who was successful in his trapping, and who then taught me how to ride a two-wheeler.

When I was young, a robin flew into my third-story bedroom and flew about in anguish, pecking at the windows and leaving his droppings. Robins are wild, I figured, and I was glad that my mother was brave enough to open the window, amidst that wild fluttering, and let the robin go. I was glad to see him go.

When I was young, I had fevers that kept me home from school. And my mother was always busy about the house, while I lay watching dust-drops slanting in the sunrays through the windows, and imagining, in the fever, that little pixies were dancing on top of the candles on her dressing table.

My mother was always cleaning around my fevers and worrying and calling the doctor, when I was young.

"Who were the boys you kissed?" my new teen-ager asked me. She should have said, "Who kissed you, Mom?"

Anyway, just because I remember my youth, and because it's none of her business, I started counting on my fingers all the boys who did or did not but had an impulse to kiss me or were not kissed back but anyway had an effect upon my life, one way or another, and when I ran out of fingers, I sent her to bed.

Sleep, little sparrow, I was thinking. Rest, nest, and kiss the bark of trees and let the rain fall upon you.

—**katey**

Tнıs is the first week of May, and an incident that happened when I was a kid, many years ago, hauntingly reminds me each year that this is the season good fortune begins smiling on me.

My father, a minister who concealed under his reverential halo the horns of a practical joker, seriously remarked one day before the first of May that there was a certain spring rite absolutely necessary for "the making of good fortune."

My twin brother and I were probably nine or ten years of age at the time. Father related there was a tradition that involved this first day of May. To incur good luck for the remainder of the year, one must salute spring at dawn on this day. He had to bare himself, go out in the buff to greet the first rays of the sun, and roll in the dewy grass . . . just as the Greek gods welcomed this joyous season. Dad pointed out that Pan sang his paean in the fields at this moment in spring, and that we should also sing our praise and triumph over the ills of the world.

It was a mean trick. We set the alarm clock, arose at its clanging early on May 1, and ran outside naked. We huddled on the porch, shivering and certainly not feeling joyous. Finally, after the first rays of the morning seemed to lift so slowly, the sun peeked over the horizon.

We dashed onto the lawn, flung ourselves prone on the dew, rolled and rolled, and, not knowing what else to sing, bellowed the old Thanksgiving hymn, "We gather together to ask the Lord's blessing . . . he hastens and chastens, his will to make known."

Uncomfortable, sodden with the cold dew and cut grass that clung to us, we sneaked back to bed. As we lay there we whispered, seeking to find from the other some sign. Did we feel any different? Was there a stirring of good fortune or even a lifting of the spirits within us, whatever that was? The only feeling we had was the cold and the wet. So, uneasily, as if there were some experience we hadn't quite savored—or perhaps we had failed in our initiation—we went back to sleep.

We didn't know that the "devil" in ministerial robes had awakened with our alarm, sat by his bedroom window, and slapped his thighs in glee as he saw his two sons rolling ignominiously in the dew. Actually, he wasn't cruel; he just couldn't resist one of his many inventive practical jokes.

However, as the first week of May visits me, I always get that feeling: I wonder, really wonder, if I shouldn't be down there in the dew, baring my skin to the sun and rolling. At least it wouldn't do me any harm . . . and there is some therapeutic good, isn't there?

Isn't that silly? But, neighbors, if by chance you do awaken too early some May morning and see a bald-headed, potbellied Pan cavorting on the lawn, it's only the spirit of me seeking the good fortune I deserve.

—ross

My mother is Irish, and I don't know why all the rest of us aren't. Lots of interesting things have happened to my mother, and I suppose it's because she's Irish. There couldn't be any other explanation.

She used to enjoy salesmen coming to her door, for instance, whereas I, having German blood in me, look upon salesmen as invaders of my privacy, enemies to progress, and that sort of thing. I even decided one day that the next time a salesman came to my door, I'd tell him that I was very sorry, it wasn't personal or anything, and I loved the cut of his suit, but I just had to make a rule not to let any strange men into the house, because my husband absolutely forbade me to talk to strange men (jealous, and all that), and besides, I had a nasty experience involving the police one time when I let a strange salesman in (that's not true, but I thought it would have a scare angle), and so on.

I wasn't cut from quite the same cloth as my Irish mother. A magazine salesman came knocking when she was up to her elbows in soapsuds, and she looked at him dumbly and sorrowfully and said, "I'd love one of your magazines, but I can't read."

He saw the glint in her eye and came back with one of his own: "That's too bad, ma'am, but you could look at the pictures."

Ah, there was a salesman! (He didn't sell her a magazine, but his ability ought to be recorded.)

Then there was the time a young and rather harried-looking fellow came with a whole case of paper products, useful in kitchens, bathrooms, and, I suppose, elsewhere in the house. He was right in the middle of his sales pitch when my mother got a beady and murderous look in her eye, leaped up from her chair, and with knees bent, arms in front of her, and a purposeful incline to her back, crossed the room and clapped her hands right in front of the salesman's face.

"Miller moth," she explained.

He left without making a sale.

—**katey**

I N the thirties, in the midst of the Depression, a horde of unemployed men—called bums, tramps, and hobos—left the South in the springtime. They traveled, uninvited, via railroad freight and coal cars and worked and begged their way north.

Along the railroad tracks they established temporary hobo camps. From these camps they scoured each town, asking for food, money, and employment. If food was scarce, they raided farmers' fields and usually procured, illegally, their favorite foods: onions, potatoes, and corn.

My father's parsonage was located on the outskirts of town near the railroad tracks. My twin brother and I loved to walk the rails, and when spring came we hopscotched down the tracks merrily and wantonly. Did you ever skip your way on railroad ties? It's the sign of spring and a young boy's spirit.

One day, one tingling spring day, my brother and I were skipping down the tracks about a half mile from our home. We came near a small grove of trees and there, grouped around a fire, were the hobos. They were young and old, shaven and unshaven, mild and violent, bedraggled and neat.

One fellow stood out prominently to us. He was redheaded, quiet, and when he spoke the others listened. (I learned later that he was a college graduate.) Red immediately took us ten-year-olds under his wing. He introduced us to "bum soup," which consisted of potatoes and onions cooked together in a tin can of water. It was delicious. He told us of his travels and encouraged the others to give us their tales of adventure, of living under the stars, moving from lush countryside to intriguing city, leading a carefree, happy existence.

Red was also our guardian. He allowed no "bum" to swear or utter any foul words in our presence. When we wanted to join the hobos, he told us of their poverty, of cold nights in freight cars, of empty stomachs, of spring rains and wet clothing, of bad companions whom no one could trust or believe, of lonely days when a family was more precious than adventure under the stars.

We invited him to our home. He came, and he was welcomed by our father and mother as one of the family.

One hundred yards to the rear of our house was the railroad. It passed by our property in a cut, about twenty to thirty feet below our ground level. For the next three years, in the springtime when the buds emerged, Red would come suddenly from nowhere, poke his head over the cut, and shout us out of the mulberry tree.

I can't explain it, but there was an eagerness in us, during those years, for spring and Red to arrive. He was kind; he was gentle; he taught us the strange ways of the world with an older brother's instinct. He brought with him a fascination, a feeling for the world without and a seeking for the world within.

One spring, without warning, Red did not come. My brother and I waited. Summer came, and we knew, we knew, but we waited. Red must have found a job, settled down, sired children of his own, and now is happy . . . I hope.

Spring pushes a strangeness into our lives. Each time it comes, there is a freshness, a Red popping his head over the cut, and it catches us. It opens our hearts to a wonderful adventure of living: the unexpected. There is this pleasure in spring, and there is a Red in everyone's life, I guess. He was a tramp, a hobo, a bum; call him anything you will. He was spring to a little boy.

He knew the last time he saw my brother and me that one more spring would make us more wise and less wondering at his ways. Spring moves on to summer . . . and it must have hurt him. It hurt us.

—ross

THE other night I heard Julie Andrews singing "I Could Have Danced All Night," and the whole bit sounded charming. I had a cold in my head, however, and an ensuing tendency to view any kind of gaiety with mild snorts of reservation.

There have been times in my life when I could have danced all night, because of my mood and the music, but every time I felt that way, my date was either a lousy dancer or he wasn't concentrating on the job at hand. Every time I encountered a good dancer and came to a rich enjoyment of our movie-starlike ability to associate well on the dance floor, he'd either start whispering inanities into my ear (and that threw my step off) or he'd say, "Let's go for a drive into the mountains."

One time many years ago—and I believe we were dancing to a nickelodeon at the Autoport—my date, just as we were executing what I considered a rather fancy and intricate step, muttered into my ear, "I'm falling for you."

I ignored his tall, blond beauty, the handsome profile, and the dark coat with velvet collar that he had worn to impress me, and I reminded him that I had been eating peanut-butter crackers before we danced, by saying, "Excuse me, dearie," and I quit dancing for a second, "just give me time to get this peanut butter out of my molars." Then I sucked at my teeth, looked up at him, smiled charmingly, and said, "Now then, you were saying—?"

(My whole vision of that incident is currently colored by the fact that I have a cold in my head. It was probably terribly romantic, or might have been, if I had allowed it.)

Another date, and a much better dancer, really did drive me into the mountains. All I wanted from him was dancing. He was very good and just my height, but he wouldn't let it go at that. He had to show off his other abilities, including the car his father had given him for college "work." What he didn't know was that I love the smell of hemlock better than dancing, and the sound of mountain springs bubbles me more deeply than a good dancing partner.

He said ruefully, "I brought you out here to get you into a mood, but it didn't work."

"It did, too," I told him. "I love it out here. You don't."

(I didn't like the idea of his using my beloved mountain springs and hemlocks for such a thought as he had. He should have stuck to his dancing.)

I could have danced all night, if my partner had cooperated.

—**katey**

Find a patch of blue 2

CHRISTMAS is no season for loneliness.

This is a simple story. It isn't important, but it might be a story of the many kindnesses that people perform in the spirit of Christmas.

I was an Air Force man during World War II, stationed in Lakeland, Florida, in 1943. A friend of mine, who had friends in Miami, was invited to spend Christmas with them. He invited me.

Very early Christmas morning, we took a train to Miami. (I must explain that this friend of mine was very young and thus unschooled in the etiquette of living.) We arrived at the train terminal and he blithely said goodbye to me, saying that he'd meet me there that evening after his day with his friends.

I was astounded. I had assumed that I was also a member of the Christmas party, not just a companion on a train trip.

I was lonely, very lonely. I walked the streets of Miami. I tried to call a friend of mine who I knew was in the Army there. He was out. I stopped at sidewalk stands and drank orange juice. I went to a movie.

It was time for dinner. Where would I go? I went

from one restaurant to another, peering into their windows, scanning the inside, unconsciously trying to find a place where there might be a moment of friendliness. I couldn't find one.

Finally I walked into a small, unpretentious place, where there were few people. I don't know why I chose this place. It wasn't attractive or appealing. Perhaps I was tired.

I sat down, and a middle-aged waitress came to me. She smiled.

From that moment, the spirit of Christmas visited me. She talked to me, asked me about my home, my life, my loves, my hopes, my destiny. She comes to me now not as a beautiful, spirited thing but as a woman of great warmth and feeling, this waitress. I can't remember what she looked like, what her tone of voice was, whether she was slim or fat, blonde or brunette . . . but she laughed and talked with me.

She spent Christmas with me. She turned my loneliness into a bright, merry holiday. She knew I was lonely, and she gave me her care.

When my friend returned from his fattening, full day, he met me at the train terminal. He asked me, "Did you have a good Christmas?"

"Yes," I replied, "a love-full Christmas." He was puzzled but never asked. I wished he had.

—ross

I T was a beautiful, clear morning in 1944, and I hated such a morning. I wanted a foggy, rainy, stormy morning . . . because it was my twenty-third combat mission, and I didn't want to face death again.

As I climbed into our B-17 Flying Fortress, I tapped the ground a superstitious goodbye and glanced at the bright blue sky. That flash of blue, when I hit the earth in a parachute, was my last memory before I woke up a captive of the Germans.

I was taken to a German military hospital, where most of my prison life was spent in a lonely hospital room. There, since I was a curiosity to the German wounded, I was visited by many Nazi patients. One of them, who had lost his mother and sister in an American bombing raid, threatened to come into my room some night and knife me.

I tried to stay awake. Since my leg had been amputated, I knew I couldn't move, so alertness was my only supposed defense. Naturally I dozed, and I awoke with a loneliness and terror that I've never experienced since. The darkness was my death.

I stuffed my head under the pillow and cried. They say a man should never cry, but there was no man's world here, no need to don the hero's mantle, no way of damming the tears. I was too weak, eighty-five pounds of flaccid flesh, and too sorry for myself.

Exhausted, I fell asleep. The next morning I looked out my window and there was the most beautiful, indescribable patch of blue that ever blanketed this earth. My small room, it stretched into infinity . . . and suddenly my life stretched with it.

I suppose there are moments of revelation. This was mine. I said to myself at that moment, "Each minute of life is an eternity, and it's how that minute is lived, how acutely one perceives it and absorbs it within his being, that determines how much a man becomes a sun: he generates or he explodes."

Don't get me wrong. From that moment I lived with as much fear, but I also lived with love.

And here's where I find it difficult to explain. It was the simple things that formed my daily pattern, and still do. To smell a rose is a casual second in one's existence, but not then and not now. Green is green, but sometimes—like today, when the rain burst upon the lawn and suddenly the sun hit the glistening blades—it is greener.

I find myself glancing back at a child's smile, reaching for a noble thought like a freshman, waiting for next fall's football games as eagerly as my son, looking to my wife's eyes for the message only she can send.

This is what I'd like to transmit to young men and women who hold anguish in their souls today. The greatest anguish, to me, is fear without hope, love without sharing, beauty without knowing. "You're too young to die . . . spiritually," I'd like to tell them. "You're throwing away the greatest birthright: a patch of blue in your soul."

—ross

W AR is filled usually with one grim moment after another, but now and then between those moments an incident shines through that transforms the grimness into a laugh-tickling episode.

It happened to me in November 1944, when I was a prisoner of war and being held in a German hospital near Vienna. For months I had been kept alone there, but an order came to transfer me to a war-prisoner repatriation center at Annaberg, Germany. Since the Germans evidently didn't care to waste a military escort on me, the officials chose a carefree Austrian "man about town" to accompany me.

It was in Vienna that I learned the kind of man he was. We arrived at the railroad station about 11 a.m., the time when American bombers usually appeared overhead. As we sat in the station, he spied a lovely Austrian lass, approached her, and propositioned her. She must have agreed.

The young guard came over to me, told me the train

would not leave for three hours, and instructed me to stay there. Where else could I go? Away he went with the lass. For three hours I sweated out the sound of bombers as they soared past Vienna without dropping a single bomb on the rail yards. He returned smiling.

Our next stop was probably an unscheduled one. It was night and we halted in a small town because bombers had struck a major terminal ahead. The Austrian took me into a small beer garden, where he plied me with beer and cheese. Again his eyes favored a young lady, and again he told me not to move as he disappeared with his new find.

I sat there as I had in Vienna, in my U.S. Air Force flight jacket, imagining all types of mayhem that some irate Germans might inflict upon me. Perhaps the beer mellowed their aggressive inclinations, but also there seemed to be only old men, inquisitive but beyond caring for any warlike displays of retribution.

He returned smiling. We stayed there practically all night and entrained finally for Leipsig . . . and, of course, arrived there in time for the usual appearance of bombers.

This time we sat on a bench outside the station. No bombers appeared, but another lovely miss did, on schedule. He eased over to her, flashed his winning personality, and away they went. I knew I had time for reflection, and I wondered about the lad.

How did he acquire such fast-acting charm? What did he say that struck such a responsive and willing chord in his ladies fair? Why did he never strike out? Did he have a medieval magic potion or was it simply his demeanor? I reached no conclusion as he returned smiling . . . wanly.

When we reached the Annaberg repatriation center, I stopped him before he left me and asked him for a final favor. Would he tell me, I asked in very halting

German, what was the secret of his success with women?

"Ich liebe!" he replied. And I guess he was right. Love conquers all, especially in his case. But as he departed I mused about his ability to dispense his love as generously on the way home.

—ross

T EN years ago tonight I was in a German war-prisoner camp, and that strange and beautiful Christmas Eve taught me that the Christmas spirit is everywhere . . . even in the hearts of lonely and dispirited men.

This was a war-prisoner exchange camp where the amputees, the blind, the terribly fire-scarred, and the seriously injured were held. The men were from many countries: England, Scotland, Wales, Ireland, Australia, South Africa, New Zealand, Canada, and the United States.

We were cold and hungry. We lived in a drafty stone building, eight to a room, and slept on straw beds. Our diet consisted of a lukewarm soup supplemented by those wonderful Red Cross packages that came every two weeks or once a month.

Each prisoner was wrapped in his own peculiar cloak of self-pity, and the only fires that warmed him were the faint embers of memory. Americans bickered with Englishmen, picking on each other for being "uncouth backwoodsmen" or "supercilious tea-drinkers." Invaluable chocolate and cigarets were stolen and each man eyed his neighbor. Two Englishmen, each with an arm missing, quarreled and staged a ridiculous one-armed battle. Two Americans, both blind, argued about the fidelity of their wives and swung wild blows.

Two weeks before Christmas a subtle change came

over the camp. The German authorities gave us the go-ahead for a big Christmas Eve party.

The lads who prided themselves as cooks got together. Actors and dancers began working out routines. The singers started rehearsing.

Guards were bribed, and the precious chocolates and cigarets were traded for eggs and flour. The amateur cooks spent hours planning a special cake. Raisins from Red Cross packages were hoarded, and Tennessee hillbillies concocted and distilled a potent brew.

I was named director of the Christmas choir. For many hours we practiced. An Australian, South African, Welshman, and I formed a quartet to sing Negro spirituals. You can imagine the conglomeration of accents that blended on "Swing Low, Sweet Chariot."

On Christmas Eve the whole camp gathered in the assembly hall. After a few skits were performed, the dancing and specialty acts were given. The enthusiastic "kriegies" made them do their acts again and again. Dickens's *Christmas Carol* was read, and the British reader's accent sounded strangely beautiful and appropriate.

For the finale, the choir of many nations took the stage. To an unaccustomed eye, it would have been a haunting sight. The director, balanced on one leg, conducted singers on crutches, one-armed book-holders, and men whose eyes could see neither books nor director. But to this audience, it was familiar and commonplace.

The songs they sang were melodies of all countries, and then the songs of all Christendom, Christmas carols. The audience joined the singers on "Silent Night" and "Auld Lang Syne." As I turned toward them, I saw all of them—the English, Americans, New Zealanders, all of them—standing there weeping. Their tears were unashamed, unnoticed. It was a precious moment, a moment in which we understood, in the music, so many unspoken words of our homes, our own special Christ-mases, our pains, and our aching loves.

When we ended with "Good Night, Kriegies," the men filed out into the night, quiet. Each one went with that deep and indescribable Christmas spirit within him . . . and the peace that accompanies it.

And I believe that the star of hope and joy, the star of Bethlehem, shone on all of us that night.

—ross

M ANY years ago I sailed the high seas in a ship called the *Gripsholm*, a Swedish liner that was being used by the International Red Cross for the exchange of war prisoners. We were amputees, blind, or otherwise sorely wounded youths who would not fight again. The scars that had been inflicted upon us were easily visible, but there were deeper, unseen scars.

We were afraid. Some of us, as we were sailing in the white *Gripsholm* emblazoned by many lights at night, sweated with the fear that the Germans would torpedo the ship . . . even though we were assured of a safe conduct across the Atlantic.

Others, like the fellow whose face was so seared that his nose and ears were practically gone and who slept with his eyes open because his eyelids were gone, wondered if wives and sweethearts would accept them as they were . . . broken, hideous, or maimed.

And still others feared themselves. They kept silent vigil. They could not face themselves as they were, and they could not find a substitute for what, secretly, they knew they were. So they banished themselves from reality, and they lived in the world of yesterday . . . when they were whole, free to move without the awful limitations of today.

Our worries were open and hidden. They were physical and mental. They ran the gamut and they were real and unreal. There was one thing in common: the mark of tragedy was evident upon each of us.

Today, filled with the goodness of living and the rewards of a loving family, I look back on that short trip across the Atlantic—when we wondered and feared—and I say to myself, "What, in the span of these years, made the difference?"

I have not kept contact with my fellow prisoners. They scattered to all parts of the nation. I imagine they moved into their villages and cities and took up their pursuits or languished in their chairs. They were rejected, loved, accepted with reluctance, or hidden within themselves until they died before they died.

I can speak only for myself. When I reminisce about those days of 1945, it is with a distinctly detached air, as if I were almost a stranger to that lad who was so intense and wounded. The fears he had then are not with me now; today's fears are far stronger and more realistic. Even the loves I have today are deeper and more binding.

I guess if I were to analyze the disappearance of my tragedy of the forties, I'd have to say that life is too filled with today for anything but a casual glance over my shoulder at yesterday.

—ross

O<small>NCE</small> in a while I take a day off and travel to Williamsport, where I get my artificial leg repaired. It takes time to whittle, grind, polish, and refashion the limb, and the hours go by slowly . . . except the other day.

As the orthopedic man began his labors, another man came into the waiting room. He had been sent there from a hospital clinic for repairs, because he had a sore stump and needed immediate attention that day. He was kindly informed that I had come a long way, I had an appointment, and he'd have to wait until this job was finished.

He sat there for more than an hour, and then I heard some feminine voices. It was his wife and probably her sister. "Why must you wait this long?" the wife demanded. "Can't you see we've been sitting in the car for over an hour, and we're getting tired?" He placated them, and they left.

After another hour, the women reappeared. "Listen," they said. "We're exhausted. Go into that room and tell that man that we can't take this much longer. After all, people must be considerate of us, too."

That reminded me of an incident that happened to me years ago. I was sitting at the kitchen table with Katey and some of her relatives. I was on crutches at the time and asked one relative if she would mind pouring a cup of tea for me. The quick Irish in her replied, "What's the matter with you? Why don't you do it yourself?"

I am pleased about both incidents. First, a handicapped or crippled person is far from recovery if he centers attention on himself so vividly that others are too conscious of his handicap. But when others push a handicap so far back in their minds that they forget, at the moment, a special need, it is a wonderful sign to the crippled that he's crossed the bridge from abnormality to normality.

I've always maintained that every cripple has a great responsibility, in order to enjoy a full life. He cannot hope, in his self-pity, to have people come to him and cross that bridge to abnormality. They cannot understand the nature, the pain, or the extent of the injury.

For instance, when I was at Walter Reed Hospital, a group of amputees would wander to downtown Washington. A "normal" person seeing them come to a swinging door would be in a quandry: should he or shouldn't he offer to open the door? Some amputees would sneer at him and say, "I can do it myself." Others would gripe because he didn't.

The ones who said, "Thank you," even if they could open the door, won a victory. They crossed the bridge. The crippled who try their best to inform the uninitiated, who silently pass over the neglect or faux pas of others, who ask for help when it's needed and accept it when it's not . . . they soon will become most normal to their friends and loved ones.

Crossing that bridge from abnormality to normality is an arduous journey, but it is one that is increasingly rewarding with each step. There's a heavy cross to bear, but it gets lighter on the way.

That's why, when I heard the two women berating the amputee in the waiting room, I felt pleased. His loved ones were showing their natural exasperation at a natural situation . . . and that's the way it should be.

—ross

3 Ah, Love, if I were king

"My mommy done told me . . ."

But I never wore pigtails.

Nevertheless, she told me, "It's just as easy to fall in love with a rich man as a poor one."

She even introduced me to one who was rich, and then I met a few others who were rich. I asked one I met on my own, "You say you earn your own money? How?"

"With stocks," he replied.

And I said, "Oh, you mean you don't really work for a living?"

And he said, "Yes, of course. My stocks work for me, and I work for my stocks."

I came from a country town, where stock meant cattle, not pieces of paper. I often wonder where he is now, that rich boy I met in my freshman year of college, that young man who told me I was so "utterly desirable."

My mommy done told me . . .

My hair was long enough, but pigtails weren't in fashion.

But my mommy also done told me, "Never let on that you know how to iron shirts or scrub a floor."

Meantime she taught me very carefully how to iron a shirt, and how to starch the cuffs, collar, and front panel, and how to scrub various kinds of floors, from the cellar to the kitchen linoleum to the oak floorboards in the dining room.

I married a poor boy, and I cooked him my mother's meat loaf, and I washed, starched, and ironed his shirts, and I scrubbed floors from the attic to the cellar. I never taught my daughters how to scrub, and now I'm regretting it. My son knows more than my daughters about ironing and scrubbing and making meat loaf.

My mommy done told me . . . no, she never told me that he'd be a worrisome thing that would leave me to sing the blues in the night. And he hasn't. It's just this guilt feeling I have about making him think he's the only one in the house who can build a proper fire in the fireplace. After I had him thoroughly trained in the building of a fire, to which he added his own good notions about how not to make the thing smoke up the house, he came in the other night and found a lovely fire going. I hauled up the logs myself, huffing and puffing from the basement, and there it was.

Well, my mommy done told me . . . never let on that you can do anything. Act helpless. Pretend that you can't wring out a cloth or carry anything heavy or see cobwebs on the ceiling. Sorry, Mom. He wasn't around, and I wanted a fire in the fireplace. And he isn't a rich man.

—**katey**

IT takes a lot to make a man cry, but here I sit with tears plopping down my cheeks like golf balls and sobs racking my chest until I feel like a steam engine chugging up that last mile of incline.

I interrupted Katey as she hung our children's yule

stockings on the fireplace mantel, and she obligingly brought me two towels before she kissed away the remnants of my cloudburst. But I must blame Katey. And I must share this rueful experience with you; it's the only balm I can think of, without another cascade flowing down my cheeks.

It started with Katey, in one of her fits of cleanliness and exploration of old nooks in our house, bouncing into the living room with a small ledger in her hands.

"Look, Ross," she exclaimed, "here's a find! I discovered this old account of 1946. It lists our daily expenses when we lived in Lancaster . . . and see. We paid only $32 a month rent for our apartment in those days."

That did it. I grabbed the ledger. She was right. But then the pain began. It originated from my hip pocket.

I looked at an entry that told me she had gone grocery shopping one day. She purchased $3.25 worth, which included a beef roast for $1.25, peaches, flowers, bread, eggs, peas, limas, green beans, and asparagus. At that moment, I began to heave slightly.

But my children tell me I'm brave. They remind me that I didn't get the DFC for hiding my head under a bombsight. So, with that mental encouragement, I read on.

On May 20, Katey had taken me on a shopping spree. I bought a raincoat for $16, a suit and a sports coat for $66, and eight ties for $8. I paid a tailor's fee of fifty cents.

A few entries later there was this cryptic remark: "stepping out, $2.40." I wondered how many drinks we had consumed. But a few notes further, I learned. Movies and a midnight snack for both of us cost $1.10. We must have had a wild, wild time a few nights before.

Since I did not return home at noon in those days, I faithfully entered the costs of my daily lunches. They were thirty-seven cents . . . day after day. Oh yes, I splurged one time, no, twice, on June 17 and 18, and squandered forty-seven cents.

One night I took Katey to the Stevens House (it was famous for its rare roast beef), and it cost us $3.20. I must have been conscious of our dining out in style, because I got a shoeshine that day for ten cents. And I paid the gas bill of $1.50 also . . . and got a haircut for sixty cents.

Thank goodness, I must have had a premonition, because my notations lasted only three months. I probably sensed that someday I'd break up over these figures.

Oh, well, as a friend of mine says as we sit down to a poker evening and I've lost my first ante, "There's not a dry eye in the house." Thank you for your concern. I wish I could be with you to furnish you with a crying towel.

—ross

"I HEARD a speech the other night," said Ross, "and the man said not to kid ourselves. It's really a woman's world, he said."

"I do not know whose world it is," I said as I tied somebody's sash, "but I'll tell you one thing or two: it isn't mine, and it sure isn't yours."

"The man said," Ross went on unheedingly and typically, "he said, 'Whose house do we visit on Thanksgiving? Is it to Grandfather's house we go? No, it's to Grandmother's.' "

"Would you like to know," I asked as I wiped somebody's nose, "why it is that we go to Grandmother's house? Even if you would not like to know, I will tell you anyway. It is because if we went to Grandfather's house, we wouldn't get a darned thing to eat."

"The man asked," Ross continued, "about whom we look at when we go to a wedding. The groom? No, the bride."

"The reason for that," I said as I wiped some nondescript moisture from my fingers onto my blue jeans, "is that the bride's wedding gown is the last decent outfit you'll ever see her in, and you might as well drink in the most of it while you can."

"It sure is a woman's world," said Ross. "The man said did we know who owned two-thirds of the real estate in this country, and we said no, and he said, 'Is it men? No, it's women.' "

"Do you know," I asked, wiping some spilled milk off the floor, "who cleans and keeps in repair two-thirds of the country's real estate? Is it men? No, it is women."

Ross was lighting an after-lunch cigar. "Women," he said between puffs, "live longer than men. Do you know why?"

"Because they haven't time to die," I answered as I crawled out from under the sofa with a mitten and hastened somebody off to school.

"No," said Ross, puffing casually, "it's because they give vent to their emotions. They cry at sad movies, things like that."

"Now that you mention it," I said, rubbing a hand through my unkempt hair, "it's been a long time since I've given vent. What's playing at the local theater?"

—katey

THE queen was in the countinghouse, counting out the money; the king was in the parlor, eating bread and honey; the maid was in the garden, lacquering her toes; along came a blackbird and nipped off every nose.

I have, as you know, deliberately misquoted a nursery rhyme because, if I can believe what I read, times have changed. Women, I'm told, control most of the money in this country, and wives are still providing their husbands with daily meals.

Also, "maids" are seldom available, and when they are, they ask for more than their employers are prepared to give them, even for social-security tabs.

Then, of course, there's the minority problem. In the rhyme I merely had the black nipping at the noses of the whites. I haven't taken any stand against or for any group. I'm just for people.

Now along comes an author with the impossible name of Lionel Tiger, beastly name, with a book that is sure to become as much of a fad as wheat germ was about fifteen years ago. The book is called *Men in Groups*, and it states that men have always enjoyed each other's company.

That isn't news to me. I've always enjoyed men's company, too, and I'm a mere female. But that's the point of the book, that our present society is still following the old saying "It's a man's world."

Right now they can have it if they really want it. I'll stay by the hearth and fix the bread and honey and then count the shekels afterwards.

I don't have a maid, and I've never met a person I didn't like, for some reason or other, black or white, and I've never seen a bird (except, perhaps, for those purple grackles that gang up in our trees and howl and mess the sidewalks) that I didn't like.

Anyway, if men want the world, they can have it. The only problem, as I see it right now, is that women outlive men, and women should therefore take some part in the world's activities, even when they grow old or otherwise become a nuisance to this world of young men.

Women have much to do with the education of their men's children, especially when those children are very young, and if our man's world doesn't present them with anything lovely, the women aren't going to educate very well.

Frankly, I'd like to write a book, without the educational background of Lionel Tiger, under the pseudonym Lioness Tigress or even Human Pussycat, to say that the world is for both men and women, and that the effect of women is even greater now than it was when men were out hunting and women were letting their children draw pictures on the cave walls.

—**katey**

I've been reading about the women's liberation movement, the one that practically says, "Down with men, and let them have their own babies."

I can see some of the reasons for this animosity, because it is a man's world in business, industry, and even publishing. Women don't get comparable pay, and promotion comes twice as hard, even if they deserve it twice as much as the men who get the raises and the new jobs.

But is this man's world the whole world?

I'm reminded of my tiny (under five feet), skinny grandmother. My first remembrance is of riding on her kitchen coal shovel as she pulled me from kitchen to living room and back again. She had a gentle face offset by steely eyes and a gruff voice.

Her two apron pockets were filled, one with pink lozenges and the other with white ones. She doled them out in firm reward for good deeds I performed, but sternly withheld them when I was a "bad boy." In later life, when I got to know her better, I likened her to Queen Victoria. She ruled the family with her eyes and her voice.

Grandmother was the only person, man or woman,

who could quell my vociferous father, make him admit his error, and bring the sweat to his active brow. All she did was peer at him and, in her husky voice, bring him to his figurative knees. She could also knight him with the same glance and voice, only this time with a touch of gentleness.

She was the ruler of her world, and there were none who contested her reign. I wouldn't term her a matriarch—she was too bending and too full of good will—but she had the fond respect due a true queen.

Now that I'm older and have rubbed elbows daily with women, I must manfully admit that they can match my wit, intelligence, industry, and logic—and even go me one better in one or all departments. I've learned that women don't need protection in these attributes; sometimes I do.

What does puzzle me is that some of these liberated women don't recognize that, within this total world, there is a man's world and a woman's world. For instance, I'd hate to see a woman competing with a weight lifter, shoveling a ditch, working a triphammer, mining coal, or fighting a war. On the other hand, father would have a difficult time bearing and nursing a child and, above all, substituting for that peculiar and wonderful element of nature, mother love.

However, my biggest puzzlement is the vow, by some of the most liberal man-haters, that they will abstain from any amorous contact with the male. Holy smoke, that's the beautiful reason we're all here. It's like relegating us to the floating pollen that drifts willy-nilly in the breeze.

As for me, what's better than having these two worlds meet and create a larger world? Actually, I couldn't resist if I tried. A woman's smile, her special glance, a meaningful word, the touch of her hand, her kiss, the way her body curves, and the thousand and one

unique things about her can come only from the wonderful person called a female.

Please, oh liberated ones, don't take that away from
men. After all, it's a man's world only if women give it
to them.

                                                    —ross

"Now see this," said Ross, holding a toy magnet in
one hand and a bobby pin in the other. He let go of the
pin and it leaped to the magnet and clung there.

"That's people," said Ross. "There's a magnetism
in their attraction for each other."

"True, lad, true," I said, "but which of us is the
magnet, and which is the pin?"

"What's the difference?" he asked.

"Makes a lot of difference," I said. "One of us leaps,
and the other just stands there."

"If you're going to go into equality of magnetism,"
said Ross, "we're going to get awfully involved." And he
tried the magnet on a safety pin that was lying conven-
iently on the table. (Any time I really need a safety pin
around here, I have to look under the couch cushions,
and that just shows that it's a man's world.)

The pin refused to leap to the magnet. No attraction. Toy magnets and safety pins do not get along
nearly so well together as toy magnets and bobby pins.
I was all set to conclude that the more a woman deals
with diaper safety pins and the less she deals with the
bobby pins essential to her hairdo, the less the magnetism.

Such a thought would have turned Ross into the
magnet and me into a choice of two, bobby pin or safety
pin, and I was in no mood to make a choice, as I was
feeling like an individual at the time and didn't care to
be catalogued. I therefore changed the subject adroitly

by remarking, "Such a business as this keeps the earth suspended in a precise place in the universe, and if anything went wrong anywhere with this tricky magnetism, you and I would not be sitting here quietly discussing which of us is the more magnetic. We would be flying off into nowhere."

To which Ross wondered, "Where is the big magnet? To what are we all leaping?"

I had a picture then of the earth viewed from the moon or somewhere—the earth as a half-lit disk suspended in space, and most of the people clinging to the surface of it, a select few flying about it, and all of them wanting to go home and not knowing where home really was.

Within such a picture, it didn't matter whether I was a bobby pin or safety pin, just so the big magnet was strong.

—katey

I HAD a good day, for no reason that I can name, just as bad days arrive unreasonably and unexpectedly. I mused, on the good day, about the connotation of the saying "A woman's place is in the home."

When women say it, they say it with sarcasm, and when men say it, they say it with vehemence and sometimes with an obnoxious air of authority.

It ought to be said with gentleness, with pride, with tender love. It ought to be said in the same way that one would say, "If I had the moon, it would be yours," or, "If I were king, ah, Love, if I were king—"

What has happened to the word *home* that modern women resent being told that their place is there, that modern men relegate women there in the tone of a judge passing sentence?

Home is the location of all our childhood memories.

Home is where Christmas is. Home is the place we get "sick" for when we are away from it. Home is a thing we build to replace the home we lost when we left it. And in the building we use the finest ingredients, gathered through the years from the home of our childhood.

Home is where birth and life and death are. Home is where we take off our shoes and take down our hair and come closest to ourselves. We reserve most of our tears and much of our special laughter for home.

Home is the place for secrets, for roast turkey, for the epitome of anger and of love. Home is full of old shoes, new wrinkles, familiar smells, fresh sheets, and visitors' hats.

When the seasons change, violets to clover, clover to chrysanthemum, chrysanthemum to holly, home is the place where our thoughts lie. Home is the place for opposites, for hurting and forgiveness, for memory and forgetting, for noise and for silence.

Home is endlessly full of the dust from which we were born, with which we live, and to which we shall return. Whether it's "home port" or "home base," it's the thing we start from and end with.

The next time someone tells me that my place is in the home, I shall wonder what I have done to deserve the best quarters mankind has devised.

—katey

Dear Ross . . . Dear Katey 4

Dear Ross,

I've been sitting across from you today, looking at your face, which I have looked at off and on for fifteen years, and I've been wondering how you would seem to me if we were strangers on a train together, sitting side by side on a day coach, going nowhere in particular.

For all I know, we might very well be strangers, in spite of all the living we've done together, and for all I know, we might be going nowhere in particular, in spite of the lovely horizons we have painted for each other.

How would we react to each other now, as strangers on a train? I think you'd speak to me first, not because I'm a woman but because I'm a human being and you like human beings, for some strange reason. You always want to be with them, no matter who they are.

You would ask simple questions first, and I would answer. Fifteen years ago I might not have answered, but your presence in those fifteen years has caused me to look up respectfully when anyone speaks to me.

You'd ask me where I was going and, being ornery, I would answer, "Now or forever?" and thereby give my soul away in a split second.

How much of our fifteen years would show in our faces? Would we look as if we had been married for ten years? Would the Big War show if you didn't get up and walk down the coach with it, displaying your limp? Would your limp show on me?

Would my eyes or the lines on my face show that I had seen your face when it was full of life, when it was under anesthesia, when it was full of smiles for the first baby, when it was angry, when it was tired of a long day, when it was anxious about a child, when it was sleeping, when it was freshly shaved, when it looked strong and protective, when it looked like a scared kid?

Would you look like any old stranger if we just met on a train? Would I think, "Gee, whoever his wife is, she's lucky"? Would I show that I'm a mother? Would you want to talk to me, and just whistle? Or would you want to whistle, and just talk to me?

What do you think, Ross? If we met as strangers, side by side on a train, would we be interested enough to pursue the relationship? Would you ask for my telephone number, and would I want yours?

I'm curious. What have we done to each other, and for each other, and because of each other?

Happy anniversary, Ross, and how are you?

—katey

MARRIAGE may begin as a bed of roses, but sometimes it turns into a bed of thorns.

Romance is the most wonderful thing in the world to the two who are about to get married, and their flowery dreams create an aura of "we were made for each other." However, there's the stark reality of making the marriage work—keeping the daily eye-openers and tiny irritants in perspective. It's difficult to scatter the dashes of romance, like scented petals, around the house when the first baby is wailing for milk at 3 a.m.

The big pitfall in marriage is that the husband or wife didn't know they had to make so many adjustments in so little time. Why didn't papa or mama "prepare me for this lunker's snoring" and "the way he shovels the food into his mouth"? Actually, they probably did, but those were the little things that would change after the wedding.

But it is those little things that most challenge wedded bliss. For instance, how did Katey know that each time I was puzzled for a quick reply, I'd light my pipe? It's an irritating stall she never counted on. Or what about my being left-handed and seemingly clumsy with the way I cut a roast, carve a turkey, or unwind a sardine can?

I can swear, after years of marriage, that it takes patience and perception to accept the daily foibles of a mate. Ask Katey.

Did she realize that I was a minister's son and had adopted the awful habit of emphasizing a point of conversation with a jabbing finger? I even tried, in early years, to sit on the offending digit when I got into a hot debate. But Katey has always managed to say the right thing, such as, "You're being a minister again."

Now, if we should consider a lifetime of these irksome things, it is a wonder anyone is married. Think of it: day in and day out, a tacky tic, a repetitive phrase like "you know," the placing of a newspaper in the same spot on the floor, a toothpaste cap never replaced, the clearing of a throat before a pontifical statement, and on and on.

There's only one positive way of looking at it: at least we're unique unto ourselves. We have our own peculiar ways of being noticed. We leave hints and trails all over the house.

Then again, I can turn those faults of mine into a good compliment. If Katey can survive all these years with me, she must be a beautiful, sensitive, forgiving person.

"Katey, please hand me your matches. I just ran out of mine."

—ross

I was telling Ross the other day that women, because their role in civilized society is still somewhat earthy compared with men's, have keener senses. My sense of smell, I told him, is almost foxlike compared with his. I find this attribute, in the machine age, more annoying than beneficial, however.

For example, I can detect the presence of a dead cigar butt at fifty paces. Ross can be right beside it and completely unaware of it.

My sense of hearing, too, I have told Ross, is keener than his. In the summertime, for instance, when insects are letting go at night, I can pick out different sounds from the complete chorus and hear them separately. Most of the time Ross isn't even aware of the chorus.

He never hears dripping faucets or electric-clock hums at night, either, unless I point them out. Then he can't turn them off as I can.

I have been cured of torturing him with such nightly observations, however. One night I informed him, as he was dozing off, that I had heard someone sneaking around in the lower regions of the house. We both sat up in bed in the dark and listened intently. The silence and darkness made me quite tense. Then suddenly, without warning, Ross shouted, "WHO'S THERE?" I was so startled and terrified that I screamed and bounced into the air, clutching frantically at the blankets. I haven't heard a burglar since.

The only sound that ever really got Ross going in the middle of the night was one that roused the entire neighborhood. Our car horn was a bit restless that night because we had just returned from a thousand-mile trip. The horn kept going off periodically without provocation.

Ross made three trips downstairs to the garage in his pajamas to stop it, and eventually wrapped himself in a blanket in the back seat to spend the night. At 3 a.m., he couldn't do anything with it. It was holding forth like a colicky baby. Ross tore back upstairs, dressed, grabbed the car keys, backed out of the garage, and headed like crazy for the nearest open gas station.

I sat in bed listening to that horn as it faded away into the distance and laughing at my mental picture of the embarrassment on Ross's face as he sailed noisily through our sleeping town, praying that some garage attendant would still be on duty.

He found one, of course. All through the next day, I went around reciting, "Listen, my children, and you shall hear tell of the three o'clock ride of R. B. L."

—**katey**

FRESH from a wedding anniversary, I asked Katey the other night, "Why did we get married?"

I knew, after living with her for so many years, that she would take for granted my romantic love for her then. I also knew that she would ponder the intrinsic reasons for marriage . . . so I popped the question.

She didn't disappoint me. "I suppose the underlying reason for marriage is a desire for companionship," she replied. "Or, to put it more negatively, there is a fear of being alone."

I was slightly shaken by her answer. Some of my friends call me an incurable romantic, and such a practical answer, even from a loving Katey, takes the stars out of marriage. Then I thought for a moment, and I admitted to myself that any yearning springs from loneliness.

While I was cogitating, Katey added, "People don't deliberately set out to establish themselves this way. There is in marriage a genuine care and love mixed with it, plus a sense of duty or obligation, but the basic, selfish need not to be alone is the one that cries most loudly."

Amen! I can't bear to be alone. I (and the "I" looms larger since Katey mentioned it) need her sitting across from me while the twilight sifts through our window, parrying my words, complementing my thoughts, lending her smile, her quick eye, and her friendship.

Katey continued, "That's why I feel that people who marry must first of all be good friends [aha!] and, if they want to continue the marriage throughout their lives, keep working on that friendship. And that nucleus will grow to encompass family and other friends."

I sat for a few moments and thought about Katey's remarks. I looked back at the years and wondered how we got from there to here, how we moved from and through our love to what we are today.

And the word *companion* came to me. There is tremendous sharing in a marriage. There are so many infinitesimal sharings: the common details of a stuck window, a broken hinge, a child's croup, a rug that needs replacing, an anxious trip to the doctor, and on and on. There are also the poignant sharings: when tragedy strikes starkly and life stands still and won't move from its base of hurt, or when geese wake us at dawn and chatter at us with their mad honking, or when the wonderful mystery of a first child envelops our waking and sleeping hours, or when, in a midnight conversation, we ease gently into an incomparable sense of one thought, one mind, one being.

Then the years themselves fade into a oneness, an infinite now, and we are friends . . . and lovers . . . forever.

—ross

THE sun was already beginning its slow descent into the west, and still Ross had not returned. I glanced up briefly from the novel that had engrossed me all afternoon (being under the impression that I ought to get engrossed sooner or later with F. Scott Fitzgerald), and I was aware of a vague feeling of apprehension.

He had not said, before leaving, how long it would take, and there was no reason for me to assume that he should arrive before dinner. Nevertheless the feeling was there, a sensation of mild panic, a premonition, perhaps, of things to come.

Nonsense, I told myself, and I also advised myself not to cross bridges before I came to them. I was momentarily comforted by the wisdom of my advice. Still, I could not return to the novel. Some nameless fear inside me kept intruding upon the pages of print.

Besides, the baby was yelling from his crib upstairs, and the other kids were getting hungry.

I put the book down and went upstairs and changed the baby's pants. My thoughts were elsewhere. A lifetime of love and travail crossed my mind briefly as I carried the baby into the kitchen, gave him a piece of zwieback to chew on, and put the spaghetti on to boil.

"What has happened?" I wondered as I set the table for the children. "Could it be that the symphony we have been composing together will end in discord by some sick circumstance that neither of us could perceive? Will the project fail? Will Ross, in spite of himself, be forced to accept defeat?"

I caught myself up short, which is easy for me since I'm not quite five-one, and remembered Ross's words at a crucial hour of the past: "Live nobly while you live. Tomorrow you may not die."

Nobly I served the children's dinner, nobly I kept Ross's dinner warm, and with a casual nobility I answered the childish query "Where's Dad?" with a reassuring "He'll be back."

As the hours sped and the sun sank fast, I pictured Ross returning, tired and disheveled, and I put myself to ensuring a cheerful homecoming by brewing a pot of tea. I would not eat, I thought, until he came.

But I got very hungry, as I always do at six o'clock, and I ate a lone and fearful meal, which was very tasty, if I do say so myself. I had just begun my coffee when I heard the familiar tread across the side porch and the familiar slamming of the door. He was home! Flooded with relief and expectancy, I rushed toward him. "Darling!" I cried. "Who won the ball game?"

—**katey**

O NE of those doomed grooms of June accosted me recently and said, "Look, you've written a bit of folderol about June bridegrooms and their marital steps on an idealistic plane, but how about a few practical tidbits?"

Okay, lad, here goes, but remember, what's sauce for one gander is grit for another.

A kiss in the morning is worth two at night.

It may be nice to have your wife bring your slippers, pipe, and paper after you've wended your weary way home from work, but after a week of accepting that servility, you'd better don an apron and help her make the salad.

After you've watched your wife pin her hair up for the first time, it might be wise to pause a moment and swallow before you blurt, "You look so different." It might turn out to be an invitation for her to visit her mother.

And speaking of your mother-in-law, don't make the mistake, even if you are very much in love with your wife, of telling her mother, "You know, after my wife, you're the second-best cook in the world." It may be an invitation for a prolonged visit to prove you wrong.

After your week or two of honeymoon bliss, when your beloved attempts her first roast for dinner, and it's either burned beyond recognition or bleeding with rawness, again swallow slowly before you comment, "Maybe you'd better ask your mother how to prepare a roast." You may lead a bachelor's life for a lonely week or two.

A man's home may be his castle, but a woman's home is her life. The lord of the castle may think that he's in charge, but his wife will let him think so only as long as his commandments don't interfere with her soft suggestions.

A man wears his hat to protect his balding pate or shed the rain, but a woman wears hers as part of an ensemble, a chord in a symphony, and the husband who choruses about "that weird hat" has sung a flat note.

A kiss before dinner is worth four at night.

The first quarrel is like two banty chickens squaring off, with no quarter given, no ground relinquished, and verbal blood flowing freely. The second quarrel, dear lad, must be fought warily, with just enough sparring and just enough battle to stir the blood—without spilling—and with room enough to retreat gracefully. If you win, you lose handily. If you lose, you win nobly.

Tears are sometimes a woman's only defense. She may cry from sheer fatigue, utter boredom, or complete frustration. If you don't know what to do—and that's most of the time—try a little tenderness. A man must learn to be tender because it comes slowly to him, but an ounce of tenderness is worth a ton of advice.

Finally, did you ever think that a woman is no more complex than you are? It's only a matter of point of view, and the strange ways of a woman may be only a figment of the strange attitudes of a man. At least, that's what you might keep telling yourself when your wife wants to eat cold potatoes and anchovies at five o'clock in the morning . . . unless she hasn't told you she's pregnant.

Of course Katey, my love, knows that I speak from acute observation of others and not from experience. And son, that's diplomacy.

—ross

IT'S very unusual for Ross to have a sleepless night. He's one of those rare persons who can lie down on a couch after lunch or dinner and doze off immediately. He can also go to sleep at night with a pre-set alarm clock in his head and wake up, as he has instructed himself to do, at precisely 7:45 a.m. or whatever time he chooses.

Most people lie in bed for fifteen minutes to a half-hour or more before turning off the day's activities and drifting slowly into a deep sleep. Sometimes people like me take even longer. I lie there wondering whether brain waves could ever be coded into symbols equivalent to written words, or whether split-second thoughts cross the mind of someone who has just been beheaded, or whether a timing device could measure how long it takes for a thought to be transferred into a verbal communication, and other peculiar ideas that are not conducive to sleep.

The other night Ross couldn't get to sleep immediately, and he was worried about it. I wouldn't have bothered with him, but he was sighing and shifting and otherwise preventing my own slumber, and I knew that if he worried about not sleeping, he'd just make matters worse.

I therefore suggested that he stop thinking about whatever he was thinking about and concentrate on something else. He asked what.

"Pick up a piece of chalk in your right hand," I said.

"I'm left-handed," he reminded me.

"I know you are. That's why I want you to pick it up with your right hand, stand in front of a blackboard, and write your name as often as you can without falling asleep."

This interesting suggestion was made in the dark of night, and I lay there wondering whether he was following my suggestion. Then, being right-handed, I picked up a piece of chalk with my left hand and began to write my own name on a blackboard. I had completed about three of my mental signatures when I said sleepily, "You don't have any t's to cross in your name, but I do."

"Quiet," he said. "You're interrupting me."

I was quiet for a minute, and then I said, "I always cross my t's while I'm there with them because I'm afraid I'll forget them by the time I reach the end of the word."

"Now you've got me working on your name instead of mine," he said.

"I don't have any i's to dot," I said. "I think everyone ought to cross his t's and dot his i's. If I were an i, I would want my dot put above me. Otherwise I'd feel neglected."

He asked if I would please shut up and go to sleep.

I did. And as far as I know, he did too. At least he looked rested the next morning, and I figure I must have annoyed him to sleep.

—**katey**

THIS past weekend a lass whom Katey and I have known since she was a little girl, got married . . . and I felt that soon, just around the corner, my own daughters will be preparing to take their marital vows. After all, they're fast getting to the age when the trip to the altar will be uppermost in their minds. Anyway, I thought—half wryly and half seriously—they'll surely ask Katey and me for the ingredients of a good marriage.

First, I said to myself, surveying the contents of my pocketbook, I'd better repair that shaky ladder in the garage. When I see the candlelight of romance gleam in their eyes, I'll take the prospective groom by the elbow and guide him to the ladder of love. However, when I speak of this suggestion to my daughters, they take me seriously and start preparing me for the rigors of pre-marriage shindigs, wedding dresses, church ceremonies, and receptions for tearful relatives and friends.

Oh, well, I console myself, I can at least give them some tips from a marriage-wise man:

Love him, I'll tell my daughter, more than yesterday and less than tomorrow.

Spoil him enough to make him mellow but not enough to make him stubborn.

When you tie an apron string around him, tie it loosely enough for him to forget who put it there in the first place.

When he argues vociferously with you and with man-made heat, remember he is only trying to convince himself that he is wrong.

The way to man's heart may be through his stomach, but the way to man's mind is through his heart.

A husband's wish to be out with the boys a night or two may be prompted by his desire to see if he's welcomed home.

The first year of marriage may be spent getting to know each other, but the remaining years are spent developing what you know.

When you have a quarrel, it takes more than a kiss to make up what you lost.

Tears may turn a man's mind away from a moot point, but you can't cry forever.

There is no great distance between a woman's mind and a man's: the trip can be made easily over a well-traveled road.

And there is no greater sharing than that between a man and a woman . . . of a sudden thought, a deep love, and a lifetime.

—ross

I'M not above getting the giggles now and then, even though I'm past the age for such nonsense and have transformed the adolescent titters into what I now prefer to call chuckles. You've had the experience, no doubt, of being in a situation that suddenly strikes you as funny, even though no one else can see the humor. You try to stop laughing, but every so often, back comes the thought you were trying to avoid, and there you are laughing again, regardless of what anyone else is discussing or doing. In most places except classrooms, this kind of humor is socially acceptable, but there's one place where it's absolutely taboo: the doctor's waiting room.

Ross and I go for a checkup every six weeks or so, for various minor ailments that crop up because we insist upon living on this lovely planet whether anyone else wants us here or not, and we shall probably continue to hang around long after our bodies have given us broader hints that we have no business doing so.

The waiting room was crowded, and one lone man moved to the end of a couch when I headed for it. People, for some reason, hate to sit next to each other in doctors' offices. I had brought a *Time* magazine along, and Ross picked up another ancient edition of something and sat down beside me. There we sat, shoulders touching, magazines in front of us, quietly reading.

I began to chuckle. "Well, here we are," I said to Ross, "side by side. Cozy, isn't it?" And I laughed again. Ross couldn't see anything funny; he tried to move over a little, probably in the hope that if we weren't so close together, my humor would collapse.

"Oh, don't go away," I said, chummily rubbing my arm against him. "It's just that we've never sat this way before, except on planes or buses or trains." He didn't react. "We should have an armrest between us." He kept on reading, hoping, I suppose, that people would think we weren't related.

We're not. We're just married. I tried to read, but somehow the two of us sitting there side by side kept striking me as funny, and I came close to whispering in his ear, "Wanna neck?" but I didn't.

Laughter, I'm told, raises the blood pressure rather than lowering it; it's a stimulus, not a relaxant. What struck me as even funnier was that after our checkups, we compared notes, and Ross's blood pressure was higher than mine. Next time we'll sit in opposite corners of the room.

—katey

Many years ago I saw a movie in which two old

people, husband and wife, were sitting together and reminiscing. They were soft and quiet, mostly unhurried. They were also contented, accustomed to each other, and full of comfort.

Great gaps fell into their conversation, but they didn't mind. He went on with his reading, and she did too. Sometimes they just sat there, not doing anything.

Then he said to her with a mild chuckle, "You know what I worried about most just before we got married?"

"No. What?"

"I worried that we might run out of things to talk about."

And then both of them laughed. As a young bridegroom, he had apparently lain awake nights trying to dream up topics of conversation that would keep them going for a lifetime. Young people who are about to choose "forever and ever" together worry about many things before they enter the strange world of marriage, but if it goes well with them, all those anticipated worries are forgotten in the realities.

Last week Ross and I drove 280 miles together without children yelling in our ears from the back seat. It must be years since Ross and I have been alone in conversation for that length of time.

We never ran out of conversational material, going or coming back. There were a few quiet gaps, but they were comfortable, thoughtful, and understood.

And what did we talk about? Of course we discussed the pros and cons of our children, but we also talked about politics ("Don't you wish some forthright Republican would be brave enough to get into the battle?" and "Do you think you can take four more years of a Texas accent?") and about music ("Ever notice that a song is good if it feels good when you're singing it?") and about being together ("The nicest thing in the world is a man and woman living together all their lives and becoming friends."").

We talked about signs on the highway, such as "CAUTION: WIDE LOAD." When we noticed that two of the wide loads we saw were preceded and followed by cars with big signs, I asked Ross, "When do they make laws about wide loads? Do they wait until there's an accident because of them, or do they anticipate the danger?"

And then we talked about anticipating dangers with regard to rearing children and general behavior, and we told each other that no matter what we fear or anticipate, some other freak thing might happen. Nevertheless, we kept the safety belts fastened.

We didn't run out of things to talk about. Spring was all around us. Trees and bushes were blooming, and so were our thoughts.

We could have gone miles and miles before losing talk with each other. But there were children waiting with their own talk for us, and we knew we had to be quiet between us, except for patches of speaking here and there and now and then, for miles and years, and we didn't mind because we'll have, we hope, someday, so much more to talk about.

—**katey**

KATEY and I were sitting in our living room the other night, and a cozy silence enveloped us. She was reading a book and I was rocking in time to a piece of music. For almost an hour there were no words between us, no exchange of thoughts, not even a twitch of an eyebrow.

I began to contemplate our mood. There are many kinds of silences, I thought, and most of them are accompanied by loneliness. However, there was no loneliness here. Some silences are awkward, contemplative, eerie, devastating, threatening, potent, holy, or awesome. But this one, seldom mentioned yet beautifully shared, is companionable silence.

At that moment in my reverie, Katey looked up from her book, saw my glance, smiled, and continued reading. There was an ease in her look, one that said to me, "Aha, Ross, there's a thought building in you, and so sit with it awhile."

The understanding gleam in her eye raised this question in my mind: where, in our years together, did the intermingling of our thoughts begin? Or was it a gradual process, one that began with tacit understandings and ended with this companionable silence?

I remembered the many times I started, in bumbling, hesitant sentences, to express myself, and Katey interrupted with a clear word to interpret my thought. Then my words evolved into a look or a gesture, and the understanding was there in Katey.

At times Katey and I begin a conversation simultaneously, and a lightning thought flashes between us, and we smile. There, in that moment, is again the quick comprehension, the sudden sharing. I feel as if my mind has flared, for that instant, into Katey's, and we grasp wholly and completely an intuition within ourselves.

There is a wonderful comfort I feel. Even with friends who know and understand me, I must reach out, seek their reaction, and search for the words that will open up our avenues of approach. But with Katey it is there, ever present.

I turned to Katey that night, and she knew that I was finished with my contemplation. She put the book on her lap and waited for my gush of philosophy.

"Katey," I said, "you know, we've got something here. Just sitting a few feet away from you, in complete companionable silence, I feel your presence, the way you look at me, you. Do you know what I mean?"

She smiled. "Maybe the silence is boredom," she said.

Why, that Irish colleen! I'll kill her, I thought . . . interrupting such a beautiful moment.

Then I saw her eyes dance. She knew. And I began to think of ways I could best her Irish wit. As I rocked, I realized it would take me a long, long time, and more silent pondering.

—ross

As I stood in church twenty-five years ago today and heard my own dry-throated, quaking responses in the wedding ceremony, there was a teasing question jiggling in the back of my mind: what do I want from my marriage with Katey?

I can answer that question much more surely today. When you marry, you're so caught up in the newness of each other that there is little else beyond discovery. It's only when the years edge upon years that one can sort out the jigsaw puzzle of living together and say, "These are my wants."

I want love, deep, enriching love that reaches further than the starry-eyed infatuation that makes the senses swim. I need the kind of love that envelops me like a blanket, warm, responsive, full of concern, and so strong that it is an armor against any adversity.

I want compassion, a tender regard for all the faults I'm trying to overcome, and a hand outstretched toward me when the day is bitter and the cold winds are buffeting me.

I want faith, from one who believes in me as I struggle to identify my thoughts and tenets, a haven when I must turn in my insecurity and ask, "Am I moving? Am I pursuing the dream?"

I want understanding. There is nothing more precious, when one is sitting in the quiet of a home, than a thought flashing to his love, and the thought being caught, quickly and fully, with understanding there, completely, in her words and her eyes.

I want laughter and good humor. When the day is long or tragedy strikes, there is the boon of a lilting smile, the turn of a phrase, and the sparkle in her face.

I want children to fulfill my days, to challenge me with their youth, imbue me with their enthusiasm, and keep reminding me of the changing pace of the world.

I want hope to crowd out the despair I sometimes feel, to raise me from the muck and mire of some dark, stormy day.

I want a rich, lovely, complete life that lifts my spirit and endows me with the satisfaction that this existence of mine has meaning, is lovely, and is graced with goodness.

All this I want . . . and have. If, when I stood there trembling at the altar twenty-five years ago, I could have asked so concisely for so much, I would have doubted. Today I am blessed. It makes me wonder at and anticipate the next twenty-five years. If this is the silver, bring on the gold!

—ross

5 Unfinished business

DURING the years that Ross and I have been filling this particular space in our local newspaper, we have probably been repetitious, but never deliberately so. We don't go through Ross's conscientiously kept file of old columns (I keep telling him that saving our columns is like trying to save a day in his life) to reprint something that was written five or six years ago, on the excellent theory that nobody would remember it.

However, I remember an old one that I wrote about Ross when we were mere pinch hitters for Lou Bell's "Once Over Lightly," the column that preceded "Open House." In it I mentioned Ross's delightful habit of juggling old clichés, putting two common sayings together in one mixed-up phrase and making it sound right to people who weren't listening carefully. Ever since that column Ross has watched his clichés, because I made him self-conscious.

It is time for a review of them now—because he did it again very recently. It took him eight years to come through, self-conscious lad that he is, and if I list them here and now, it will probably be sixteen more years before he does it again, but it's worth the risk.

Here they are, as they have come to me and others down through the years:

"The poor old soul has a tough oar to hoe."

"I have no bone to grind with him."

"He didn't mince his bones about it."

"Lovely wedding, and sentimental, too. The two mothers stood around with tears in each other's eyes."

"She yielded an iron hand over him."

"He's a hail-weather, fair-met sort of guy."

(At the bridge table) "This is a six-hand if there's a day."

"He did it faster than you can shake a whistle."

"Our childhood days are lost beyond compare."

"You have too many fires in the pan."

"Well, keep your ears peeled."

"Take the horns by the reins."

"He certainly speaks legibly, doesn't he?"

"You'll make me so self-conscious that I won't pull any more of my purest rays of gems."

I didn't though. The other day he told me to "turn the shoe off on the other foot."

I would if I could and willingly, but I'm so dull and literal and unimaginative that I've been examining my feet ever since, very soberly, and I've decided never to wear shoes again.

—katey

Most people have stock phrases that become almost characteristic of them. I said "almost," and I have a wish that no one will neglect that little word, because so much of experience is "almost."

One man I knew from my little lifetime said over and over again, "I'll have nothing but silence, and very little of that." I liked that sentence because, simply, I like sentences like that.

James Stephens, in *The Crock of Gold*, wrote dialogue for a woman who couldn't decide between two men who were apparently panting for marriage. The lady said, "I like one as well as the other and better, and I'd just as soon marry the one as the other and rather."

My father was forever saying, "Do this immediately, if not sooner."

Someone else told me that I was "tautologically redundant," and I liked that. I'd have liked it just as well if he'd said that I was redundantly tautological, besides being repetitive. (Oh, go look it up. I did.)

Anyway, one of my stock phrases, and it's rather recent with me, is, "I don't care what anyone does." I do, of course, but I figure if I tell people that I don't care what they do, they'll let me alone to do what I want to do.

For example, the kids will ask if they can go here or there or do this or that around the house, or maybe Ross will ask me if it's all right to play bridge here or there or anywhere around the house, and I usually say, "I don't care what anyone does."

Give them enough rope, I figure, and they'll let me hang myself.

That reminds me of some advice my sister gave me years ago: "Give a man an inch, and he'll take it." Isn't that loverly? I mean, that he'll take it.

Some clown on TV said that he and his wife had never had children. "It's hereditary," he explained. "Chances are, if your parents never had kids, you won't, either."

Mine did, and you might know I wouldn't have enough imagination not to follow suit. Of course not. It's hereditary.

Are you following me? If you are, cut it out. If there's anything I can't stand, it's someone hanging around and peeking over my shoulder every time I'm reading something interesting.

—katey

Do you have any pet peeves?

Actually, it's difficult for me to add up my pet peeves, because they are so momentary. They come in a sudden flash, then with a quick irritation are gone and forgotten.

However, yesterday afternoon a car-driving incident on campus made me think of pet peeves and, on the way home, I conjured a small list that I'd like to share with you. It may stimulate you to get a few off your chest during an evening's conversation with your husband or wife. I even thought up a few antidotes that might save you the effects of high blood pressure or a punch in the nose.

Pet Peeve 1: Have you ever driven to a four-stopsign intersection, sat and waited your respective turn, started on your legitimate way, and found an extra car charging through the intersection while you slammed on your brakes to avoid a collision?

Antidote: Smile, point your finger gently at the faulty driver, and say, "After you, Alfonse." Of course, I've never had the spontaneous generosity to act this way.

Pet Peeve 2: You're in a busy line of traffic and your motor stalls. Despite all your efforts, the balky engine refuses to start. The fellow in back of you leans belligerently on his horn and yells, "Get your damn fool car off the road."

Antidote: Casually get out of your car, saunter to the affronted driver, hand him your keys, and ask in a wistful manner, "Would you mind starting my car?"

Pet Peeve 3: You're talking to someone. As you progress in what started to be an interesting conversation, you notice he has a faraway look in his eye and is uttering a vacant, "Uh-huh, uh-huh, aha, oh." You know his mind is on his Aunt Minnie's money in Detroit.

Antidote: Stop talking. Grab him by the hand, shake it vigorously, and say in a loud voice, "Congratulations. I knew you'd accept the chairmanship of our drive. You're just the man we want."

Pet Peeve 4: Conversely, there's a man at a cocktail party who has been telling you about his father, mother, sister, brother, cousins, and aunts. As you make your tenth excuse to move and for the tenth time he grabs you by your arm or lapel for another relative story, beads of perspiration swamp your frustrated brow.

Antidote: Take his hands gently from your anatomy and say, "Pardon me, please, but this coat belongs to my brother, and I'm afraid it's getting worn in one place."

Pet Peeve 5: A man comes to your door, asks you if you're interested in education, and says he's conducting a very important survey. You invite him in, and he takes several minutes to inform you he's a salesman. You spend, as a hospitable person, at least five to ten minutes getting him to the door.

Antidote: As you get his foot out of the door, give him this parting word: "Don't bother coming back for another survey . . . you've given me an education of a lifetime."

As I mentioned, these pet peeves disappear as suddenly as they reappear. But a friend of mine reminds me, "Don't give up all your dislikes. After all, if you can't hate some little things, how can you love big things?"

—ross

"I DON'T often," remarked the wrong side of myself,

"look people straight in the eye when they're talking to me, because all too often their faces gradually turn into animals or birds of one type or another, and it makes it hard for me to concentrate on what they're saying." The other side of me is a bit abashed to confess such a thing, but I always console myself with the thought that there's nothing new under the sun, and therefore if I've turned people into birds, they've probably turned me into one, too, and I become sufficiently worried about what kind of bird I am to desist, momentarily, from this interesting conversational pastime.

"Nevertheless," my wrong side insists, "there's one fellow in particular who is composed of an avarice that slithers out of his eyeballs when he's talking to me, and before I realize what's happening, his nose gets longer, his ears disappear entirely, his forehead slopes backward, his hair turns into feathers, his eyes become beady, his neck lengthens, and I am finally staring at a vulture."

After an experience like that, it's usually a relief to turn to the magpie on the other side of the room. Any well-balanced party includes at least one homey old reliable magpie. If not, sparrows can be found pecking away all over the place without much regard for their location, and I've always enjoyed the naive crust of them.

When people turn into animals right before my sensitive eyes, the effect on my psyche (or whatever it is that makes me feel as if I'm going down too fast in an elevator) is much less devastating but just as disconcerting. I've known a charming bulldog for years and years, and you'd think, after all this time, that he'd stop being a bulldog when I stare him in the eye, and be himself. I also know a fellow who's big enough to be a grizzly and certainly acts like one, but every time I look him in the eye, I realize that his mother, or maybe his father, was really a teddy bear and that he's merely trying to live it down.

Of course, we've all known the "cat" type, and because I've become personally acquainted with a couple of real cats, I think human beings have done them an injustice. The trouble with real cats is that they're too close to being human: they have a dark side and a light side. But most of the human cats I run into perform for me only on the dark side.

It's a good thing that I'm not allowed to carry on like this for more than two pages of type, because goodness knows what kind of bird you've turned me into already. Spare me the details. And don't look me in the eye when you think that.

—**katey**

I AM not a clotheshorse. For many years my compatriots in Old Main regarded me as that dumpy little man with baggy, crumpled pants and drab coats. My constant distinguishing feature was a pipe in my mouth—and the billowing smoke clouded my friends' vision of my uncolorful suit and unshiny shoes. After all, I was comfortable; why should I make myself uneasy in natty, pressed attire?

In addition, I had an aversion to shopping. I didn't know what colors matched or what style fitted my short frame, and time spent in a store would be better used in reading and watching ball games.

So I relied on Arnie Kalin. I'd race into Kalin's haberdashery, mutter to Arnie that I needed a hat or raincoat, he'd reach to a rack, pick out an item, and I'd say, "I'll take it." Time: two minutes. As I was exiting I'd sing, "What a friend I have in Arnie."

But a few years ago my sartorial life began to fall apart at the seams. My daughters matured with an acute sense of beauty, respect for all colors of the rainbow, and a feeling of responsibility that these attributes were lacking in their old man. They looked at me with an expression of wonder: how did I exist in this modern world with clothes that reflected hobo life in the thirties?

Then I noticed some subtle approaches—and gentle reproaches. At Christmas I received what I thought were daring shirts and ties. I put them in the far reaches of my closet, but the next day they were on my cedar chest. A few beguiling smiles and urgings later, I was wearing the adventurous combinations.

The next year, when I needed a few suits, my daughters surreptitiously supervised my departing from the solid blues. I acquired light browns, minty greens, and a striped suit that has turned me into a "handsome devil" who draws continual admiring glances from my family.

Now I'm a captive. I'm a slave to their fashionable fancies—and I can't quite explain how I've been transformed or why I no longer feel self-conscious or uncomfortable sporting spring and fall hues.

For example, I'm going on a trip and I needed a summer suit. Yesterday my daughters and Katey dragged my half-reluctant self down to Kalin's again. "Two minutes," I muttered from habit. They selected a green suit for a beginning. "I'll take it," I said. They surveyed me, consulted, argued, and denied me. Then they asked for a wilder pattern, and I cringed slightly. I tried it on and they led me to the mirror. After a moment's reflection, I felt my youth returning. "I'll take it."

Oh, my daughters, what have you done to me? I lost my head—bought another pair of trousers, a shirt, tie, and belt. And, in a final fling, I grabbed a straw hat—

which I would have never considered a year ago—and bounced out of the store.

So here's a warning to my Old Main friends. Take a second look behind my cloud of smoke. You will see a rainbow.

—ross

My leprechaun is hopping mad at me again. He claims he has to be somewhere in my vicinity, wherever I go, just because I discovered him in Hort Woods on campus one day long ago. He says he can't trust me out of his sight—a very illogical point of view on his part, but there's no talking him out of it.

He's mad at me because an Irish airline is paying Ross's expenses for a trip to the Emerald Isle, and I wasn't invited to go along. If I had been asked to go, my leprechaun, who hasn't been there since I first met him thirty years ago, could have had a free ride.

"Your trouble, Katey, me love," he told me (he's forever telling me what my current "trouble" is, as if I didn't know), "is that you're only half-Irish and therefore ill-equipped to put sufficient blarney to the man. There he goes, flyin' off to the old sod, where I dearly want to be, and you sit back on your wee backside and let him go."

"Stop calling me your love," I said, "and cut out the fancy language. The trouble really lies with the ilk of the Irish men in charge of that airline. They have some peculiar notion that all American men like to take trips without their wives; that's why they didn't invite me."

"Not so, me darlin'."

"And don't be callin' me your darlin', either. You don't mean a word of it."

"What's wrong, me dearie, is the cost of the thing.

They know you'd be askin' for fancy treatment, besides
wantin' t'visit every pub in sight."

"That's not so. I'm a teetotaler."

"See what I mean, me love? Not enough Irish in
you. Oh, to think what I'm missin' because of you!"

You know, when his face gets red with frustration
and mixes with the green that spills out from his eyes,
he's one awful, bilious sight to behold. I told him so,
but he stuck out his tongue at me and disappeared. It
really isn't my fault. Ross didn't want to go without me,
but I said if one of us had a chance, it was better than
neither of us, and I'd just as soon it was he and not I
and sooner. I don't make much sense after a visit from
that leprechaun.

—katey

Is there a stranger in your life who passes you day by
day or week by week, and he or she lends a bit of
mystery or satisfaction to your world? There have been
several such strangers in my life. Some I have later met,
and others have passed me by forever. Let me give you
an example.

Each day at the corner of our street near the campus, a car draws up and a man gets out and bids his
wife goodbye with a fond smile. She drives off, and he
walks down the street toward his work at the university
. . . I presume.

He is a distinct person. You would notice him easily
in a crowd, with his graying red hair and mustache. I'd
call him distinguished looking, because he has an easy,
natural grace in his walk and bearing. The first moment
he stepped from the car, the first moment I saw him, I
said to myself, "Ah, there goes a man I'd like to look
like."

Then the conjecture began. Really, he resembles a

warm Dean Acheson, the former secretary of state. Does he teach on campus? What kind of personality does he have? I have never seen him frown as he strolls by our house.

One day as I returned from my office and entered the driveway, he also was coming off campus to meet his wife, waiting for him at our corner as usual. I ventured a smile and a wave, and he returned it with good grace. In fact, it was a charming greeting, one that I somehow expected.

He seems to have an encompassing regard for life. As he walks—and he walks like a man strolling through a woods—he glances all about him, nicely and thoughtfully. Maybe that's why his wife drops him off at our corner. He wants those steps to his office as steps into life.

This is the strange and pleasurable interlude I experience each day. I meet a stranger going his way, walking briefly through my life, and he furnishes me with a smatter of intrigue and wondering. He reminds me of other strangers I have encountered. They, too, have given me a fleeting look at themselves . . . and I have an eerie feeling that somewhere around each corner of our living there is a rendezvous, a chance meeting with someone, where there are no words, only silent greetings and an invisible hand reaching to mine.

So, as that gentle man strolls by our house tomorrow, I'll place my fancy upon him, smile, and say, "There goes my distinguished fellow again, and all my good wishes go with him, because he gives me a moment of pleasure."

—**ross**

THIS Monday, Memorial Day, we Americans will honor the dead. We'll lay flowers on graves of our loved ones, veterans of wars, and other persons who live in our memories.

It is a fitting gesture. Sometimes the dead are too soon forgotten, and their influences in our lives pass away with the years. However, this sentiment is true also of those who are living, those who have carved a precious niche in our life patterns and have made a unique and profound contribution to who and what we are.

So on Monday I'll make it a special "living Memorial Day" and give a mental rose to each of these individuals who have been an integral part of my life:

To my mother, who smiled her way through poverty, tragedy, and impossible circumstances and gave me the philosophy that love is the strongest force in the world . . . and hate the weakest.

To my father, who shared his extensive library with me and introduced me to Emerson, Carlyle, Thoreau, and scores of other authors who stimulated my young mind.

To a boyhood friend who shared and practiced high ideals with me, when both of us thought we were going nowhere and college was out of sight.

To an "uneducated" grocery-store manager and a high-school teacher who, after I was three years out of high school, urged, compelled, and needled me to come to Penn State with only seventy-five dollars in my pocket, for a try at a college education.

To a college professor who housed me rent-free for three years, acted as a father, fed my body and mind, and got me my first job.

To other college professors who opened the doors of knowledge, inspired and stimulated me, and taught me what my father's library couldn't.

To a flight engineer on our Flying Fortress crew who, when our plane was on fire, crawled to its nose where I was crippled by flak and—despite the second-by-second fear of explosion—dragged me to the escape hatch and shoved me out.

To a German military-hospital superintendent who smuggled, cheated, and tricked in order to keep me alive while I was alone in his hospital, with the knowledge that if he were discovered he would be dead.

To a newspaper editor who was as gruff and hard as any pictured in the movies, but who treated me like the son he never had . . . and gave me the soundest advice I've ever had.

To people of this community, scores of them who, through the years, have bestowed the unspeakable beauty of friendship and concern that has nurtured my love of this town.

To my children, who have graced me with their youth, vivacious ideas, and humor.

To my wife, who has shown me that love is everlasting and continually growing, and who has made my life so meaningful that my heart is too full and my voice too small to express my gratitude.

To all people who by a small deed or thought have enhanced my being, crowded out the frustrations and evils of the moment, and made my day-by-day existence a pleasure.

—**ross**

In a way, I'm a very considerate person. If I were to die suddenly, my survivors would be faced with so many messes that they'd be too busy to grieve for my passing.

Before they could shed a tear, they'd have to take a mop to at least three of the nine rooms in the house in preparation for the usual onslaught of grief-stricken relatives, who are notorious for their ability to distract themselves from their grief by counting cobwebs and peeking behind paintings on the walls.

My business is never finished, either. My survivors would have to answer pertinent and urgent mail even before my plot was chosen, and they would have a terrible time organizing it, since my filing system extends from the cookbooks to the top of the television to the desk in the den to notes near the kitchen telephone.

I have often thought of arranging my small affairs in such a way that anyone with an ounce of intelligence could walk in and take over at the drop of a heartbeat, but life is always one jump ahead of me. It is, on the whole, stronger than I am.

Any time all nine rooms are simultaneously in perfect condition for a funeral, I am, unfortunately, in excellent health and quite unlikely to fall victim to a fatal accident.

When the children are clean, hair and ears included, their nails cut, their teeth filled, their shoes polished, their drawers and closets neat, and the hamper has been emptied of dirty clothing, the desk is well arranged, the house neat and shining, and my nails filed, I sometimes think, "This would be a most opportune time to die, opportune for everyone but me."

But would it really? I'd be leaving them with nothing to do but bury me, and they'd have to concentrate on that. No. It's much more considerate to go on in this disorganized and littered way. I shall leave them with a great deal more than grief to fuss with, and work is such a wonderful antidote to grief.

—katey

Ross accused me the other day of displaying an occasional gloomy outlook on life, and I told Ross that his main trouble was that he never investigated gloom sufficiently to discuss it with authority.

He said what did I mean by his "main trouble," that he didn't have any "main trouble," and he wished I would not get into these moods in which I could see only the seamy side of life.

I said that it was my feeling that one has to wallow around in gloom for a while in order to grasp its full import and that the trouble with him was that he never even went wading in it for fear of being drowned, and he said he hadn't been having any troubles until I pointed them out to him, and I said that if he could see himself from the gloomy puddle I was in, he'd sure know that he had troubles.

The trouble with me is that whenever I'm immersing myself deliciously in gloom, I always look out and see Ross standing cheerfully on the shore of the gloom, and I have to swim ashore so that I can belt him. Only when I get there, he's loaded with cheerful logic.

For example: people are no more tense and unhappy these days than they ever were. They are just more interested in the tensions of their own age than in tensions and problems of the past. Take Ross's Aunt Clara, who is sixtyish.

Nobody who knows Aunt Clara would make the mistake of going up to her and saying, "How are you?" because Aunt Clara would take half an hour to tell you how she is, and you can bank on it that she isn't well. Aunt Clara has been sick for twenty-five years with one fascinating ailment after another, and she knows her insides as well as her outside. She aims pills at certain spots on her insides in the same way that she applies lipstick on the outside. If she were suddenly turned inside out, she would lipstick the inside and develop ailments on the outside.

She's the one who says, "It never rains but when it

---

pours," and she's the one who advises that we should never discard, but merely "lend," used baby clothes because you no sooner discard them than there you are with a new baby.

She says, "Now that you've washed your car, it'll rain for sure." And she says, "Yes, it's a nice day, but I wouldn't be surprised if we'd have rain before it's over." And she's the one who always says, "Better take your umbrella. If you don't it'll rain." She can always be counted on to sigh deeply and remark sadly and wisely, from deep inside of her, "Well, that's how it goes."

It must have rained on most of Aunt Clara's picnics.

And Ross, who knows his Aunt Clara and knows enough of gloom to stay out of it, says calmly, "Let it rain."

—**katey**

Last night I gritted my teeth and smiled through my tears.

I'm speaking figuratively, of course, because how often does a grown man cry . . . except in rare moments of great stress? However, such moments do smack a man in the prime of life, such as when his fly rod breaks with a sixteen-inch trout on its leader, when his first daughter marries, when a jack fails to work with a flat tire twenty miles from help on a dirt road in the middle of nowhere, or when he's finished riffling through the Christmas bills on a cold January night.

I must admit that those presents glinted pleasantly under the Christmas tree, that the local merchants did not coerce my family or me into buying anything beyond our yuletide desires for our loved ones, and that each purchase was reasonable and needed. But how come all our needs push upon each other at one time of the year? It's that rascal Santa Claus. He's the fellow who dreamed up that insidious tradition of a Christmas list, and he's even conjured the practice, through his magic, upon little ones who don't know any better.

There all the packages lay on Christmas morning, and they bestowed abundant joy upon us as we unwrapped and exclaimed how we had wanted this item, the next one, and the next, until our yule hopes were filled.

Now my pockets are empty . . . but the song plays on. At least the memory keeps me from crying out loud.

The bills are stacked here on the table before me, row on row, and I can't get enough courage to take the advice of an old friend of mine: "Ross," he said with the cheerfulness of a man walking his last mile, "I've worked out a method—after many years of January pain—that will ease your financial burden . . . temporarily." He paused with the import of a man who had the cure for this peculiar affliction, then said, "Here's the solution: take all your bills in your best hand (my left one is the strongest) and throw them up against the wall. Sift out the ones that are face up, since evidently they are psychically influenced by the most eager merchants, and pay those bills. Let the others wait until February. After all, you may be feeling better next month, and your creditors probably will still have left a little of the Christmas spirit and good will in them."

In case my creditors are worried about my trying this delaying tactic, I must confess I raised the bills in my fist, aimed for the nearest wall, but didn't have the guts to follow through. I lost my pitcher's toss some years ago.

So I'll sit here for a few minutes, smile through gritted teeth, fill my pipe contemplatively, puff a few minutes to delay my torture, and begin writing checks. Katey told me years ago that tragedy is only 10 percent of life, but it comes in concentrated doses. I'll concentrate on her philosophy as I begin scribbling and hold back the tears from staining the checks.

—ross

Of beginnings, middles, and ends

6

"COME now, Dad, you're not going to make another crazy list of resolutions for New Year's Day, are you? After all, you either break all of them or forget which ones you made and dream up new ones as the year goes along."

I got this stern admonishment from one of my daughters . . . who missed my point entirely. Why shouldn't resolutions be broken? That's half the pleasure of making them. The other half comes from forgetting them, wiping the slate clean in order to write down a new list of forget-me-nots.

So here I go with ten new resolutions—and the knowledge that Father Time has enough trouble keeping track of his own march, never mind mine.

1. I promise my family, unequivocally, never to use any words I cannot define to them in a quick minute. (In case you're interested, my dictionary informs me that *unequivocal* means not ambiguous, sincere.)

2. I resolve to keep our den clean, the books dusted, and papers in the desk in neat array, if my daughters

wash the dishes daily, vacuum the living room, keep their rooms in order, and iron their clothes. (I think that's the best resolution I've made for years.)

3. I vow to keep my voice calm and low when I'm scolding our children, if they, in turn, won't treat me with an anguished, all-knowing, "You just don't realize, Daddy" retort.

4. I will keep my temper when my daughters take the car without leave, on one condition: each time they forget to inform me of their sojourn, they are automatically grounded from driving for one day. (I can foresee the tears running copiously down their cheeks and their pleading eyes asking for an exception "just this once.")

5. I shall, I shall, I shall remember my wife's anniversaries and my mother's birthday with an appropriate gift. There are no strings attached to this resolution except that my florist, who has these dates in his little black book, better not have a lapse of memory, too.

6. I promise never to purchase my son any more of those do-it-yourself kits, thereby saving him frantic moments of hunting a lost piece and preventing me from gluing wrong sides together.

7. I swear by the few hairs on my balding head to get out of my rocking chair, which is located next to a warm fire in the hearth, and replace that burned out light bulb in the bedroom, fix the cracked window that lets cold wind sift into the cellar, and finish that month-old letter to my Oklahoman brother . . . tomorrow.

8. Hesitantly—and with great sadness—I will suppress my cornfed puns and humor to rare moments when my loved ones are ripe for indulging my whimsical witticisms, but they must be courteous enough to give me one last chance when they make me face the family's firing squad.

9. I promise my neighbors that my snow-covered walk will not be the last one on the block to be shoveled,

but at least they can return the favor by allowing me to be the next-to-last one.

10. Finally, while I'm in the forgetting mood, I firmly resolve to dissolve all personal enmities, wash off all grudges, forgive all petty injustices that I've fancied were done to me during the past year . . . and start all over in forming new personal grievances.

I hope that I won't have too many to forget next year. Well, at least they would form a good base for new resolutions.

—ross

I AM middle-aged. Although I don't quite know how I got here, there are certain signs that tell me I have arrived . . . reluctantly.

It isn't the total realization, you know, that makes you middle-aged-conscious; it's the insidious little things like . . .

. . . when your daughters dance lightheartedly in the living room, you tap your toes without the inclination to get up and shake your hips.

. . . when, on a brisk fall day, your son invites you outdoors to toss a football and, after a few heaves, you inveigle the neighborhood kids into a touch game and quietly fade into the house.

. . . when you weigh 130 pounds, the same weight as thirty years ago, and discover that what was formerly all muscle is now located in the jowls and nicely forming potbelly.

. . . when you see a beautiful young lass sauntering down the street and, instead of muttering to yourself, "Boy, is she a looker," you say in fatherly admiration, "Hey, she looks just like my daughter."

. . . when you reflect, in wonder, where those last

ten years went—and what's more, you don't remember where they did go.

. . . when your wife sighs to you, "Yea, even the hairs of thy head are numbered: one, two, three," and your children exhort you seriously, "Daddy, please, why don't you try a toupee?"

. . . when you climb four flights of stairs, starting out like a youngster with winged feet and ending up on the landing puffing and huffing like a steam engine.

. . . when you look at a recent photograph and there are the lines, the telltale lines of your face, revealing the erosion and the hidden tragedies of life.

. . . when your daughter—college stimulated— speaks of a burning hope, an ecstatic moment, a quick sharing, or a falling leaf, and as she waits for your equally passionate reply, you say knowingly, "Mmmmmh."

. . . when you impatiently wait out a rock 'n' roll concert in your living room, thinking to yourself, "Where, oh, where is music today, and how, oh, how did it get there?"

But there are compensations to my balding and graying thoughts. I asked my daughter last night, "What is it about me that makes you think I'm middle-aged?"

"Middle-aged? Daddy, I look at you as you are, and age doesn't come to my mind."

"Ah," I said. "Ah." And the years left me, and I was young, oh, so young.

—ross

O NE night my daughter said to the entire family, of which I was the only one listening, "Did you ever notice how a person starts out in life as a small string of a thing," and here she gestured as if she were making a string that swelled in the middle and then faded back to what it was in the beginning, like threading a needle, "and then goes up in the middle of life, and then fades back down?"

I said that of course, I had noticed, and I told her that when I was her age, I wrote a kind of doggerel poem about the subject. I lost her interest because she was watching the Academy Awards show, with which I can't compete. I therefore penciled the poem as nearly as I could remember it, because I wrote it more than twenty years ago, before I even knew about old age or anything else.

It goes like this, put into consecutive lines rather than in the form of a poem:

"One creeps, Two wobbles, Three walks; One gurgles, Two babbles, Three talks; Four shows off, Five has a pout, and Number Six's teeth fall out.

"Seven and Eight are very quiet; Number Nine should start to diet; Ten and Eleven discard their toys; Twelve is awkward, fond of boys.

"From here on the fun begins, 'til Thirty winds up holding twins; Thirty-five renews the diet; Thirty-nine begins to sigh at handsome younger men, and Forty's teeth fall out again.

"And so it goes, on up the scale, to Number Sixty, growing pale. Here the wobbling starts again, with babbles for another ten.

"Seventy-five crawls into bed, and Eighty lies there, stiff and dead.

"Now here the story ought to end, but somehow no one can depend on women's never marrying men, to start the whole darned scale again."

I would not have remembered that verse if my daughter hadn't told me what she learned about beginnings, middles, and ends. I had to explain that many forty-year-olds still have their own teeth, and that she has a great-aunt, past eighty, who is waltzing around her own house as if she were a teen-ager, and that people past the age of seventy don't necessarily crawl into bed.

You have to remember that I wrote that verse twenty years ago or more, and that medical science has made it out-of-date. I also wrote it from a female viewpoint, and my remarks therefore don't hold any water at all for males. They die younger.

—katey

SOMETIMES I feel like a motherless chile.

Remember Jimmy Durante in the movie version of *The Man Who Came to Dinner,* and the first lines of a song, "Did you ever get the feeling that you wanted to go and the feeling that you wanted to stay?"

I get that feeling. I want the comfortable shoe of the past and the strange, indistinct fit of the future, the ease of an old friend and the excitement of a new one, the swing of my rocking chair and the swift surge of a jet plane.

This feeling doesn't happen often . . . actually, rarely. It's a poignant hesitation between what was, what is, and what may be.

I sit here—lost for awhile—and I feel lonely. There are many hands reaching for me, hands so familiar and hands so strange, wanted and unwanted . . . and voices, and faces, and thoughts.

I'm in a never-never land, too indistinct to be frightening but too gray to be comfortable . . . maybe between here and there.

Ah, me, it must be the first full flush of spring that's stirring me. My grandmother used to give me sulphur and molasses to rid me of all of winter's slushes and quicken the sap that was flowing in me. I wish she could dish out her peculiar remedy now; it might lift the mist from me.

"For, lo, the winter is past, the rain is over and gone; the flowers appear on the earth; the time of the singing of birds is come, and the voice of the turtle is heard in our land."

I guess my senses are adjusting to the merry month of May, which, I'm told, originated from the Latin word *majores,* meaning "older men." The Romans believed that May was the month sacred to the majores, or older men, just as June was sacred to the juniores, or young men.

Well, then, young ones, please be tolerant of us older men, floundering from a long, numbing winter. The birds are nesting; the blue, yellow, and white violets, jack-in-the-pulpit, anemone, hepatica, forsythia, and dogwood have bloomed; the sap is running; and we older men are reacting, slowly but surely, to the half-teasing, half-tender song of May.

—ross

HEARTHSIDE

Share and share alike 1

A WOMAN's place is in the home. I don't care what she does with her extra-curricular hours, if any.

But her place is in the home . . . scrubbing the floors, cooking the meals, changing diapers, washing the wash, chasing the kids to school, scrubbing their ears and other dirty spots, washing the dishes, and handling the other thousand tasks that crop up each day.

As a man who previously had quietly told his wife that housework looked simple, I'll eat every word. I should know.

Day before yesterday, Katey was ordered to bed by the doctor, and I manfully told her I'd take over the household duties. Let me warn all men of greater fortitude and strength than mine that this great reserve of yours will disintegrate under the broom handle, the kitchen range, and the persistent voices of your beloved children.

Cheerfully, yesterday morning, I called the three children from their beds: Janny, of second grade, Kassy, of kindergarten, and Amy, the two-year-old. I told Janny to get dressed and shoved the other two pajama-clad youngsters downstairs.

Breakfast: I made several mistakes. I forgot about Janny. While I was in the midst of preparing bacon, scrambled eggs, juice, and toast, Janny appeared unclad. A loose tooth, she informed me, had to come out, and she had spent the precious pre-school minutes trying to eject it with pliers.

I told her I had no time for such nonsense. That was my next mistake. A loose tooth, I learned, is of utmost importance. I spent five minutes rectifying my error and turned to ladle the eggs . . . which were burned. The toast was hard, and the other children were complaining that they were hungry.

Janny was shoved out the door, munching her toast, but she returned a minute later for the kiss I'd forgotten. Then the rest of the morning was spent trying to catch up with that fast-moving clock.

The children were clothed, the beds made, the wash washed (only after I called on our neighbor to explain the mechanics of the automatic washer), and many other tasks completed that I'm too tired to recall. At frequent intervals, the youngest persisted in being taken to the bathroom . . . always at the busiest moment.

The breakfast dishes were just being started when Janny appeared, asking for lunch. I was beginning to reach the shock stage. Cans were opened, the contents heated, and milk was spilled . . . by me. I found myself, usually a calm person, shouting orders: "Janny, five minutes before school! Kassy, the car's here for kindergarten and you haven't eaten your soup!"

I yelled to the little one to stop sopping her bread in the soup and drawing patterns on the clean tablecloth. Her reply: "I can't; I'm only two."

The afternoon passed. I don't know how. But I'm proud of my dinner. Of course, the aforementioned neighbor provided the Spanish rice casserole, salad, and cake. But I did the hard part: bread and butter, milk, and ice cream.

Yes, I put the children to bed after bathing all three. I think I missed their ears. But the peace, the beautiful peace of solitude and quiet, that followed . . .

And may I, in retrospect, pass on a word of wisdom, hard-gained, to that calm, certain husband returning from a hard day's work: "A woman's work, grave sir, is never done."

—**ross**

I'VE just been taken for another long ride.

Our seven-year-old, who has been dropping baby teeth like snowflakes lately and charging me the fairies' inflationary price of ten cents per tooth (I used to get a nickel), just confessed with a sly, toothless grin that she doesn't really believe in those fairies at all, that she said she did only to keep her coffers filled. She has also known about the Easter Bunny and Santa Claus for some time and has kept quiet because she knew she'd get more loot if she played dumb.

"Tee-hee," she giggled, "how could Santa fly around to all those chimneys in one night?"

I said, "Okay, smarty-pants, you're now in the hole to the tune of thirty cents. Figuring back three teeth ago, on a conservative estimate, at ten cents per tooth you owe me thirty cents. Cough it up."

"I don't have thirty cents," she wailed. "I spent all my tooth money on popsicles."

Then she went on with the logical explanation that the fairy had twice failed to appear during the night and that only after she had informed her mother of this tardiness did she finally find the dime under her pillow at lunch time.

I said that if she had as many wayward teeth to keep track of as I had, she wouldn't complain about such negligence. I told her about how I had inadvertently sucked one of her sister's teeth into the cleaner just because it looked like a foreign object there on her dresser, and how I had developed a terrible inferiority complex about my status as a mother after the reaming out I suffered as a consequence, and that I ought to sue all my children for extreme mental torture.

She said, "How about the time my loose tooth was knocked out at school by Charlie, and I said it was worth fifteen cents because it got knocked out, and I only got a dime?"

I said that dead teeth were still worth only a nickel, whether they fell out or got knocked out, and that she was still in the hole, and where was my thirty cents?

I'll never get it back. I know that. And her kid brother has at least twenty more teeth to drop, and by the time he gets around to dropping them, the price will probably go up to twenty cents per tooth. Some kids are already getting two bits for molars, and I can't see that molars are worth any more than incisors.

I have a special leprechaun, an old friend of mine, and I mean to discuss this inflationary payola trend with him one of these days. The trouble is that I see him only when I see rainbows, the kind I make when I'm hosing the driveway or the kind I see when the rain falls after a thunderstorm and the sun and rain come upon me together.

But he's getting old, this leprechaun. Prices for loose teeth and fantasy are too high for him, too, these days, and he's fading out. However, he did tell me that even a slightly dishonest grin, provided that it was accompanied by a nearly toothless upper gum less than eight years old, would be sufficient to keep his rainbows shining.

—**katey**

For some reason American adults have turned over a large portion of the Easter season to their children. For that reason, you'll have to forgive me for the following words on the subject.

It all started when our seven-year-old, who knows darned well that there isn't any Easter Bunny but likes to pretend that there is in front of her sisters, asked at the dinner table last night, "How does the Easter Bunny color his eggs? The same way we do?"

"No," I answered, "I'm sure he doesn't do it the way we do."

"Maybe he has a special machine," she went on, glancing wisely and secretively at her two younger sisters.

I was slightly annoyed with this sense of superiority, and I said somewhat tersely, "No, I'm sure he doesn't have anything to do with machines."

"Well, where does he get his colors, then?" and this time, her face had more innocence in it.

"I believe," I answered, "that he must get them from rainbows. Whenever he sees a rainbow, he scoops each color into a separate little pot and saves it for coloring Easter eggs."

Age seven thought that over. Then she said, "How does he boil the eggs? Does he have a stove?"

"No," I replied, "I don't believe the Easter Bunny would slave over a hot stove."

"I know," age five cut in brightly, "he boils them from the sun."

Age seven looked skeptical. "The sun isn't hot enough."

"It is too," said five. "It's so hot on the sidewalk in the summer that I bet the bunny has to hop on the grass."

"But Easter isn't in the summer."

"No," I put in, "but the closer you get to the sun, the hotter it is."

"But the bunny can't fly," said seven, looking a little defeated.

"No, but he can hop from cloud to cloud," I continued relentlessly. (Age seven doesn't believe in pixies the way I do, and I am sometimes irked by this.)

"And—" said five, feeling her weight, "I know why he gives so much candy away. Because he has more than he can use, and he wants to get rid of it."

It was then that I felt defeated. All along I had thought five was on my side with the pixies and the Easter Bunny, and then she turned out to be a pragmatist after all. Ross was taking in the whole situation by choking with laughter on a mouthful of lima beans. I suppose we were being awfully serious.

Anyway, children aren't too different from adults in their beliefs: skeptical and suspicious one day, full of belief the next. I'll tell you one thing, though. On Easter Sunday we're all going to be believing in a lot of things, things much bigger than the Easter Bunny.

—katey

THEY didn't have "sharing time" when I started to school many years ago. I was the shy type, and I doubt if I'd have had the nerve to share anything. I know that I didn't have the crust my daughters have.

Their interpretation of the word *share* is to show off. They "share" new socks or sweaters, new hairdos (such as an occasional ponytail labored over by their mother), or a doll some kind relative has given them— in other words, something they think someone else doesn't have, and I don't mean ideas or mental discoveries.

We tried a song-sharing session at the dinner table one night, with the wild hope that the kids might learn something about music and teach each other new tunes.

Three-year-old Amy started things off by reciting rather than singing, "Jack and Jill went up the hill to catch a pail of water." We let that go. Then eight-year-old Janny, not from any sense of patriotism but because she wanted to think of a song her sisters didn't know, belted out "The Star-Spangled Banner" in six or seven different keys.

Ross, who is an agreeable fellow with a nice tenor, tried manfully to join her, but his pleasant smile was fairly sick by the time he came to "the home of the brave."

Meantime, six-year-old Kassy had been thinking hard all through "The Star-Spangled Banner." When it was over, she turned on her dreamiest smile and asked, "Do you mind if I choose a long song?"

Who can't resist the innocent smile of a six-year-old? Who but a couple of naive, unsuspecting parents? Given permission, she got up from her chair and began, "There's a great big wheel a-turnin' in my heart," with gestures.

Ross, relieved that "The Star-Spangled Banner" was done with, joined Kassy immediately, without gestures.

"In my haw-awr-art!" they bellowed in one chorus after another, moving from a big wheel to a little wheel (with less active gestures), to a big drum, a little drum, a big pump, a little pump, and finally to a great big bell a-ringin' in their hawrts.

About halfway through the fourth stanza, Amy, who had been momentarily spellbound, suddenly broke forth with, "She'll be comin' round the mountain when she comes," and Janny, feeling thoroughly upstaged, began counting the stanzas on her fingers.

Janny: "This isn't fair. She's had four already: the big wheel [holding up her index finger], the little wheel [holding up her middle finger], the big pump [fourth finger]—"

Ross and Kassy (undaunted): "In my haw-awr-art!"

Amy: "She'll be drivin' six white horses when she comes!"

Janny: "And now a big bell, and then I suppose a little bell—"

Ross and Kassy: "There's a little bell a-ringin' in my hawrt—"

Katey: "Aren't your hearts pooped?"

Amy: "We'll all be there to meet her when she comes—"

Share and share alike, I always say.

—katey

Ross inadvertently came forth with a formula for bringing up children the other day after one of ours had just received a smack for an infraction of the rules and one minute later was being fondly cuddled.

"Sock 'em and rock 'em, I always say," said Ross from behind the little person on his lap.

He was not trying to provide the world with a formula, but it sounded sound to me. Since it would not apply to offspring of all ages, however, I tried to refine it a little.

From about age two to age seven, one can "sock 'em and rock 'em" and get away with it. During babyhood, however, one can rock but not sock, and therefore I feel that "curse them and nurse them" would be a more appropriate slogan for that age group.

"Curse" is a rather strong word, of course. Maybe "cuss 'em and buss 'em" would be better. From seven to nine, one can neither sock nor rock since both are beneath the growing dignity of a child in that bracket.

There's no reason why one can't "shove them and love them," however.

After nine or ten, a person doesn't like to be shoved around any more, and therefore, from this period through the teens, one can merely "hiss them and kiss them."

When the time comes for offspring to leave home, one should willingly "send them, befriend them, and lend them." The lending process, if one has opportunists as offspring, can go on until a parent becomes too ancient and arthritic to carry on.

There are compensations for the latter days of parenthood, however. One can sit quietly debating with himself about which is greater, how much he "spends on them" or how much he "depends on them."

I would imagine that when one reaches his last days and looks back philosophically upon the whole process of propagation, with the knowledge that all men are alone, he might sum it up as he should have summed it in the beginning: "Conceive them and leave them."

—**katey**

THREE little kids
  they lost their ids
  and they began to cry.
Oh, Mother, dear, we sadly fear
our ids we have darned near irretrievably lost.
WHAT? LOST YOUR IDS,
YOU NAUGHTY KIDS?
Now you shall have no pie.
Mee—OWWW!

And they didn't get any pie, either. Here we are, knee-deep in apple weather, and no apple pies. Maybe we're only ankle-deep, but anyway, the good apples are available. The good ids aren't.

What used to be apple-pie weather has now become good virus weather, and "mother dear" sadly steers herself toward the medicine cabinet instead of the flour bin. Some sneaking germ has entered the household and made vicious little blobs of protoplasm out of my normally healthy kittens. If they had lost their mittens, I wouldn't bat even the eye that winks more easily than the other.

I have enough mismatched mittens in all sizes right now to start hooking a rug, but entertaining three sick kids of assorted sizes is a good enough excuse to get out of such other dull pastimes. Mind you, I have nothing against hooked rugs. I like them. I'm just not in a mood to hook one. My kids' ids have been hooked by a virus, and that accounts for my mood.

They're not *really* sick. They're *cranky* sick. What their ids need, I suppose, is a sizeable chunk of homemade apple pie. The way to a child's id is through her stomach or her sense of homey smell, and what smells better and homier than baking apple pie?

Of course, if this pie is to take a therapeutic turn, I'll have to let them mess around with the pie dough, regardless of the state of my own id.

The three little kids
they found their ids
in a mess of apple pie.
Oh, Mother, dear, see here, see here,
Our ids we have momentarily recovered.
WHAT? FOUND YOUR IDS,
YOU LOVELY KIDS?
Then sit down and eat your own messy pie.
Me—YIII!

—katey

FOR the past few months I have been engaged in

violent conversations with our one-year-old son, who takes up a large part of my time and therefore provides me with numerous reasons for not appearing in public or wearing hose and heels.

These conversations remind me of Lewis Carroll's "T'was brillig and the slithy toves—."

Our son, waving both forefingers like an orchestra conductor, says, "Schaw-bush mum-ne-da-da boo," and I answer, "Ishkebibble dewoten-doten to you, too, you old knucklehead," and he smiles and says, "Ho-ho-ho," as fatly as Santa Claus.

I try to throw him with some double talk I learned in college, "Steer stassin blassfus," but he waves the fingers and comes back with "Nashim stashu sh-sh-shee."

These conversations interest him a great deal more than they do me, especially the humorous veins of them (I can never figure out why he's laughing), and I'm always the one to change the subject by going off somewhere to do something.

What interests me is that I could teach him any language under the sun, if I knew any language but English. Whenever he says something that sounds like a word I know, I say the word I know, and sooner or later he'll learn to repeat it and know its meaning, I certainly hope.

I could invent a language if I wanted to, and teach it to my son, if there were any point in doing so. The first word the wee ones learn, unfortunately, is *no*, and they live with it all their lives. I could teach him *nein* or *non* just as easily as *no* but it means the same in any language. Thus far, the word *no* is merely a form of communication to this boy. He opens the bread drawer, looks up at me, shakes his head, says, "No, no, no," and transfers the bread from the drawer to the kitchen floor.

By the time he's two years old, the word *no* will be

emphasized with a smack or isolation and thus he will learn the significance of communication.

Nobody knows what a human being ought to be taught. Nobody really knows. Parents teach their offspring to do the things that they admire and not to do the things that interfere with them. What we admire in our own generation might not be admired in the next, and thus we will be accused of errors. By chance our boy, now beginning the struggle of communication, was born of American parents who speak only one language, and speak only out of their own experience, and probably do not speak well of themselves.

Thus our son is automatically limited in his efforts to communicate; meantime, however, the gobbledegook conversations are very pleasant, and while he's indulging in them, I'm all for the NOW of life, and the heck with the "blassfus" that was yesterday or the "steer stassin" of tomorrow.

—**katey**

T HIS is the season for tenderness toward the little people.

Everyone is supposed to swell up like Santa Claus and pat little heads and try, by blood, sweat, and tears, to drop answers to all childlike requests down a mythical chimney on Christmas Eve.

I have four of these tender little people in my house, and the evidence of their presence is constantly obvious. They've kept me hopping so much that thus far I haven't had a chance to buy a Christmas card, let alone mail one.

That old phrase "Children should be seen and not heard" went out with the one-horse sleigh. Ours are seen, heard, and rammed into the marrow of our bones.

Our baby was sick last week and required much cuddling by day and by night, much extra activity on our part, much denial of sleep. Meantime, the normal activities of the other three went on as usual, but with more intensity since the illness of the littlest one put their own special needs into sharp focus.

Toward the end of the week the baby seemed to be recovering, and I seemed to be more wilted than usual. To put it crudely, I had had it. There was no spirit in me at all, let alone that of a yuletide nature.

The baby by then had decided that while he was ill, he had a good deal going in the cuddling department, and he was determined to keep it up for as long as he could while in the recuperative stages.

Because I view life from an adult and somewhat routine standpoint, I consider the hour of 3:30 a.m. a good one for renewal of one's spirits, yuletide or otherwise, by blissful sleep. Our son, being young and inexperienced, had other ideas. And in a way, his stand on the question had some spirit. After all, what difference does it make what time it is when you finally come around to being seasonally tender toward the little people?

Ross crawled out of bed at 3:30 a.m. and, knowing that my mother-love instincts had reached a dangerous low, began walking our son up and down the hallway while singing in a muted, breathy, but very pleasant tenor.

He did not sing the usual lullabies. Not Ross. "Car-o-li-na mo-on, keep shi-i-nin' " drifted to my ears as I sank deeper into my pillow. Then came "I'm forever blowing bubbles" and "When it's moonlight on the Colorado—"

I dozed off completely to the personal message, all for me, "With someone like you, a pal so good and true," and I don't know how long Ross sang to our little one, but I woke up the next morning with my spirits renewed, the yuletide ones included.

—katey

Not the days but what goes in them 2

Whatever happened, I asked myself as I removed a bottle of vinegar from the baby's fists, to my love of bicycling? Gracious, I thought as I pulled the baby's head out of his diaper pail, I remember bicycling twelve miles one day and then going dancing that night.

Come to think of it, where, I asked myself as I stopped our five-year-old from sitting on the new couch with a piece of bread piled a half inch with jelly, is my old zest for dancing? Why, I thought as I slipped the baby into his highchair because his sister had given him a whole banana without consulting me, there were times when I could have danced all night.

Oh, la-de-da, the times I could have danced all night!

Where, I wondered as I raked the leaf mulch off the flower beds and chased the baby halfway down the block because he had lost interest in the raking of leaf mulch, is my love for the great outdoors?

Goodness' sake, I thought as I removed mud and

small pebbles from the baby's mouth, I used to cook hamburgers over an open fire with such zest.

Oh, la-de-da, the zest I had!

Where, I wondered as half a dozen giggling little girls filed past me and my typewriter and headed for a tray of apples in the kitchen, is my love of making verse? Why, heavens, I thought as I removed an apple core from the dining room rug, I used to sit by the hour writing verse.

Oh, la-de-da, the verse I wrote!

Have I "arrived," for pity's sake? (Why do women say, "for pity's sake"?) Is this what the zest, the zip, the energy, the soulful thought, have come to, for crying out loud? (Why do women always holler, "for crying out loud"?)

Oh, the energy I gave to the love of rough bark, to the smell of outdoor smoke that clung to my clothing when I undressed at night, to the feel of running, to smiles, and to the soft and gently tattered shadows of moonlight.

Whatever happened to all that la-de-da?

Stop coddling those downy-haired kids, I tell myself as I sweep grass from their Easter baskets for the tenth time. Why, for pity's sake, I think as I pull the covers over a small, sleeping child, they're handing you the biggest old la-de-da you ever ran across.

—**katey**

"COME and sit down on the couch beside me," said our six-year-old, Amy, to her two-year-old brother, Robby, "and I'll read you my preprimer."

"Otay," said Robby, wiggling up on the couch beside Amy and putting his thumb into his mouth.

Amy opened the book to the first page.

"Look," she read.

Robby took his thumb out of his mouth. "Gook," he said.

Amy turned the page. "Look, look."

"Gook, gook," said Robby.

"Oh, oh, oh," Amy read from page three.

"Oh, oh, oh," replied Robby.

Patiently, Amy turned to page four, reading, "Oh, oh, oh, look."

"Oh, oh, oh, gook," said Robby.

"Shut up," said Amy.

"Shu' up," said Robby.

In the kitchen I was thinking, "There's four years' difference between them. They should really abandon this farce of trying to be understood by each other."

Now take adults like Ross and me. There's nearly four years' difference between us, and the last thing we'd ever do is try to understand each other. We're too adult for that.

For instance, the same day Amy read the preprimer to Robby, I had planned earlier to do the grocery shopping during the noon hour, but my neighbor started to have a baby that day, and naturally I had to take care of her two little ones until the sitter arrived.

Therefore Ross volunteered to come home a little before five and do the marketing with Janny, our oldest, so that she could push the cart for him, because he's still on crutches and can't push a grocery cart.

When Janny came home, she said she had already promised a friend to go bike riding, but she'd be back in time to shop. Meantime, Ross called and said he'd be home a little earlier to avoid the traffic, and Janny wasn't home, so I called on Kassy, who was upstairs cleaning her room because I told her I wouldn't take her to see *Tom Two Arrows* the next morning if she didn't. She had a friend with her.

Kassy said she'd be glad to push the grocery cart if

her friend could come along, and meantime Amy came in from a neighbor's house and said she wanted to go, too. I suddenly pictured Robby, who loves to go marketing and ride in cars, left behind when all those kids went off with Ross, and I decided that one of the bigger kids could put him into the cart and that he wouldn't be nearly so much trouble in a grocery cart as he'd be hanging on my skirts and howling while I cooked dinner, so I put his wraps on him.

Just as Ross entered the house, Janny came home from her bike ride with her friend and insisted that they go along because the job had been given to her in the first place, and Kassy said she and her friend had been given the job, too, and while they were all arguing the question, I went into the kitchen, where I dusted my fingers with flour so that I could roll up the noodle dough and get it cut because it was nearly five, and you can't cook homemade noodles too soon after cutting them, although it really doesn't hurt them a bit. It's just the idea.

It seemed to me that the situation was clear and needed no handling. All the children, obviously, were going to the market with Ross. Any adult, even one four years older than I, could size that up in no time.

That's why I was puzzled when Ross, who was standing on his crutches in the open doorway, hollered for me to come back, as if I were somebody's flunky or something. I patiently and somewhat imperiously, I must admit, cleaned the flour off my fingers and returned to the scene of action.

"What sort of arrangements have you made for me?" Ross asked.

"Take them to the store," I replied.

"All of them?"

"Of course."

As they were piling into the car, another of Janny's

friends arrived, and she crawled in, too. It was very logical, but Ross didn't see it that way, and I wonder if it's the difference in our ages or his lack of experience. I'll tell you one thing, though. We're too adult to tell each other to shut up. That isn't polite.

—katey

"Hey, Mom, you got a safety pin?"

"Of course not. How ridiculous can you get? Do I have a safety pin? Indeed not. I have four kids but no safety pins. The only two safety pins I have are currently holding your brother's pants up, and DON'T YOU DARE TAKE THEM!"

What's more, I don't have a paper clip, a rubber band, the button that came off my raincoat last week, one more bobby pin, a pencil, Scotch tape, band-aids, or straight pins. I should care. The kids don't know where their jacks are, either, not to mention their supply of marbles, stones, checkers, baseballs, and skate keys.

I once arranged all these miniature objects into little envelopes and placed them neatly in a catchall drawer in the kitchen. I was in a well-organized frame of mind at the time. But the kids wouldn't put up with it. They're squirrelly. Squirrels are forever caching things away here and there, and then when they really need something, they forget where they put it.

I'll tell you how I know that kids are squirrelly. The other night they suggested that I play a game with them, whether the idea turned my stomach or not. They said I should mention some object in the house, and the first one to get back to the kitchen with it would get ten points.

I was doing the supper dishes at the time, and it occurs to me now that this game was a clever way of avoiding helping me. Anyway, they trapped me there, and I decided to think of something so hard to locate that I'd get them out of my hair and ears for a full fifteen minutes.

"Go get me a safety pin," I said.

Within five seconds they were all making running slides into the kitchen, each with a safety pin. I was perplexed.

"Go find me a paper clip," I told them.

Once again, they were back in no time with paper clips, and they performed equally well with thumbtacks, marbles, crayons, pencils, jacks, bobby pins, and buttons.

Suspiciously, I said, "Without going to my sewing basket, bring me a straight pin," and when they brought them, I said, "Go get some more," and they brought more, and I asked them please to put them into my straight-pin box in my sewing basket, which they did.

"Where did you get them?" I asked.

"Found 'em," they answered.

The point is, if they wanted a safety pin at a given moment, they'd be yelling, "Hey, Mom, you got a safety pin?" But when they're playing a game, they can apparently pull all sorts of things out of their ears, just to rack up ten points on their score.

Either they're squirrelly, or I'd better do some spring housecleaning.

—katey

I saw a "poor mother" cover picture on this week's *Saturday Evening Post*, depicting mother collapsing on the couch as her three neatly dressed children boarded the bus for their first day at school. Her toes were wriggling as she sipped her coffee, and she was savoring "this beautiful moment, this sublime hour, this whole exquisite day" when peace came and she dived on the divan. All right, all right, all right. "Poor mother," I'll say to all of you, but where's old dad?

He's putting in a hard day after the eve before. He didn't have time to wriggle his toes or collapse on the divan with a warm cup of coffee to soothe his jangled nerves. And he hasn't had time to recover from the night before, when the house sounded like a noisy schoolroom with an absent teacher.

Dad came home the night before like an unsuspecting bull driven to the slaughter. Fatigued and wet with hard-earned sweat, he innocently stepped into a whirlwind of household activity. His wife, with her arms full of dresses, muttered an absent-minded "So you're home." Where else would a conscientious man be? His daughters, all three of them, greeted him as an interloper . . . no, not interloper; errand boy would be more like it.

Before dad had a chance to inquire about the disappearance of his favorite pipe, he answered the telephone five times for squealy inquiries about who takes the bus where, why can't my daughter take the bus at another location, and whose school serves lunch. Dad didn't know the answers. What's more, the answers he did give were proclaimed incorrect.

The eve before school became increasingly hectic. At dinner dad tried to tell mother, at repeated intervals, about his one problem, but he was involved instead in several debates going on simultaneously about what dress should be worn when. Again he was wrong in all instances.

Like Dagwood, dad tried after dinner to find some secluded spot where he could rest. Upstairs, downstairs, from kitchen to bathroom, he moved . . . and each time, he was reminded that if he didn't get out of the way, school would not be reached in time, and why didn't he make himself useful. Getting out of the way and making oneself useful at the same time is quite a feat, and dad wasn't superhuman.

The eve became more frantic as bedtime drew near. Dad became the person who must find those things that had become lost . . . the great seeker, he. Upstairs, downstairs again. After all, he couldn't perform the major duties, the necessary and expedient chores; he was the doer of little things, like combing washed hair, settling minor quarrels, carrying dresses here and there, telling one child that she would like her new school, and—oh, you know, the detail man who picks up where others leave off.

Dad was also the "get to bed" guy who warned the children for the sixth time that they'd get the back of his hand, and then sat on the bed to tell them of his days in school and calm them into sleep.

The morning, the big morning, came. Dad, lulled during vacation-time into expecting quiet minutes in the bathroom, found himself evicted three times while his daughters performed their hurried ablutions. It didn't matter to them if his face needed repeated lathering. After all, "We've got to get to school."

Oh, yes, the routine of getting to school will come. The excitement will diminish. But old dad stumbled off to work with a glazed look . . . and coffee in the pot nine days old couldn't remedy that day of days.

Let's give mother her credit. Dad couldn't have performed the hundred and one duties of getting the children ready for school. But remember: mother was ready for the big day. Why didn't someone warn poor dad? He wasn't.

—ross

W HAT I know about time and relativity could be put into my thimble, and I never use a thimble.

I do know that it isn't the days that matter, but what goes into them. Ross left town on the first day of school this year, coincidentally, not deliberately. He was gone only two and a half days, but his oldest daughter apparently experienced so much during those few days that it seemed to me as if she had been gone, not Ross.

She and her father had an unexpected, chance meeting at the high-school football game after those days of absence, and the young girl was so overcome with joyous affection that she would have wept upon seeing her father, but her friends were there, and she therefore choked back the tears.

Now, part of that emotion lies in the fact that they met in a place alien to both of them, and quite unexpectedly. It was a combination of the surprise and the strangeness of their surroundings. The father had been physically away from home, although not mentally, because he has lived long enough to keep the ties tugging regardless of the distance or the time.

The daughter, on the other hand, had never left home, at least to her own knowledge, and had been in a state of excitation over the newness of strange buildings, rooms, hallways, lunch hours, new clothes, and the first football game of the season.

She was off in left field, hammering unknowingly at her own loneliness. Then, suddenly, in an unfamiliar and exciting place, she saw her father's face, and the tears welled within her.

For her, those few days were eternity. For Ross and me, they were routine. I don't know about Ross, but I feel at the moment that I could rocket myself to Venus and not be a bit surprised to find one of my children raving excitedly in the brush and suddenly bursting into tears upon seeing me.

Well, God help the kids. There are places they'll

have to visit, relatively soon from now, where they'll never see their parents' faces, and it will take them time, relatively speaking, to learn that "home" is not a place but an all-too familiar and beloved face, glimpsed suddenly in the unfamiliarity of eternity.

—**katey**

I took my after-dinner cup of coffee out to the side porch, and I sat there by myself looking around, looking at all the houses and trees and signposts that were already familiar to me. It was a moist October evening, warm, dusky, full of the wetness of a recent rain. The sky was clouded and there was no evidence of the setting of the sun. A gray day was merging into a dark night, quietly, hushingly, as if no brightness had ever been.

The marigolds in my flower bed suddenly became sharply outlined in the dusk, almost like stars on a clear summer night. In the sunlight of summer, their color had been obscured, diffused by the hazy light, but now, with the sun gone and day melting into night, they sparkled like single jewels against their dark green leaves that had become as black and soft and mystic as velvet.

I looked at them as if I had never seen them before, as if I had planted them without any awareness of them, as if I had watched them all through the softly diffused summer with its warm, filtered light, as if I had never seen a marigold.

That same day I had spent a rainy morning alone in the house, and around noon one of my little girls came home. She walked into the hallway in a red plaid raincoat glistening with raindrops. There were lots of buttons to undo on the raincoat and as I unbuttoned it, I found a shining little face under the rain-wet hood, and two eyes that glowed like marigolds in the dusk.

I looked at her as if I had never seen her before, as if I had conceived her without any awareness of her being, as if I had watched her all through the summery, diffused light of mother love, warm and filtered and almost pure, and hazy, as if I had never seen a little girl before.

When I planted the marigolds, I was efficient and matter-of-fact about them. They were designed to "spruce up" the property. I had no idea that in the dusk of a gray October night they would suddenly reveal themselves as living jewels to be reckoned with, to be counted as important.

And when I efficiently and selfishly decided to have another baby, to spruce up the property of my own being, I had no idea that Amy would shine all by herself, like a marigold in the dusk, little and bright and eager and restlessly alive, under a rain-wet hood.

I am overcome at the moment by marigolds, October dusk, and two bright blue little eyes. Any time now I shall concede my own being to marigolds.

—**katey**

O UR seventh-grader has been exposed to the first home-ec. course of her life. I've been exposing her to home ec. all her life, but nothing I exposed "took" until now.

"What are we having for dinner tonight?" she asked sweetly.

"Roast pork," I replied distractedly.

"Well, at least, we won't all get beriberi," she announced, like a dietician checking on her assistants.

I dropped the potato I was peeling, turned toward her with my jaw momentarily paralyzed, and then inquired, from the depths of my nearly fifteen years of three-meals-a-day-at-a-hot-stove, "Just what do you mean by 'at least'?"

"I mean," she replied, positively upright with self-confidence, "that at least one of the essential vitamins will be in our meal tonight. Now then—" and it required great dignity on my part to keep from clobbering her with a pot—"what else are we having?"

"Applesauce," I replied.

She considered my answer carefully and intellectually and then said, "That's fine, but have you managed color, texture, and food value in this meal?"

"Look here, dearie," I said, brandishing my paring knife in front of her upturned miniature nose, "suppose you set the table right now, and when your dinner is served, examine it for color, texture, and food value, and if it doesn't meet your requirements, COOK IT YOURSELF!"

When we began our dinner, she was still carrying on high her newly discovered home-ec. knowledge with such remarks as, "Oh, yes, the tomatoes and lettuce in the salad add color, and the green beans do, too, and the texture of the mashed potatoes is different from the meat and beans and salad, and—"

"—And also from the applesauce," I put in, but she went on with an admonishment to her three-year-old brother, "You must eat your beans for protein," and he did, for heaven's sake.

Obnoxious as her critique of my cooking was, I can't help but be grateful when I remember how hopelessly I tried to get her to eat broccoli and liver when she was four and slightly anemic, and how deftly she manages to trick her brother into eating the very things she loathed at his age.

Apparently kids won't take mother's word for it

until the word is verified outside the home. I wish the outside world would verify a few more good things besides diet.

—katey

L ETTERS! I get stacks and stacks of letters:
"Dear Mom,
"Do you love me. I love you. Sign here . . . . . . yes or no. Whats your favorite dish? Mines Roast Beff. Is yours? Sign here . . . answer. If it isn't Beff what is it?
"Love, your daughter."
"Dear old daughter,
"Answer to first question is yes. I love you, but I can't take your spelling.
"As for my favorite dish, it sure isn't Beff. I never heard of Beff. I have no favorites and this is probably an indication of a weak character. However, I can spell.
"Love, Mom."
I get letters very late at night, too:
"Dear Mom,
"Your probably going to be feragesh because I got into your bed. I'm very sorry but I couldn't resest it. I hope your not to mad.
"I LOVE YOU SO DON'T WORRY ABOUT THAT.
"Please don't be mad. And YELL, PLEASE.
"Good-night. A kiss for you.
"Love, your daughter."
"Dear Daughter,
"Kindly correct all the places in your recent note that are marked in red crayon, and if you do it properly, I promise I won't get feragesh.
"I would also appreciate knowing exactly when in the past you have seen me get feragesh [furious] and what I looked like at the time.

"Every time you get into my bed instead of your own, you are very hard to remove, and if you do it ONCE MORE, I will not only get terrifyingly feragesh, but I will beat you within an inch of your life.

"Love, Mom."

You'd think, with all the Christmas cards that come into the house, that household stacks of letters would diminish, but they don't. They get more ferageshly piled up as the big day grows nearer, and it's no wonder I haven't mailed my own cards.

—**katey**

I WAS talking recently to a young girl who works with nursery-school children and never knows whether to laugh or scream in frustration at their activities.

She told me about one three-year-old young man named George who, when he first attended the school, refused to use the toilet facilities, even at times when it was apparent to everyone that he was in great need to do so.

One time one of the teachers, noticing his usual predicament, asked him why he wouldn't use the bathroom as the other children did. He looked up and announced with finality, "Because toilets are ridiculous."

On another occasion he was discovered flushing crayons, drawing paper, and other playthings down one of the toilets. One of the teachers, who, of course, was not allowed to clobber him or even speak to him roughly, said sweetly, "Now, George, don't you remember that Miss So-and-so explained that we shouldn't put things down there because the toilet will get clogged up and won't work?"

"Yes," said George, as he continued his interesting pursuit. "That's why I'm doing it."

One of the teachers' jobs is to train the little ones to put things away before it's time to go home. George was being cajoled into doing his share because George does not like to put things away when he's finished with them. Who does? Teacher was in the middle of her gentle speech when George raised his hands and interrupted with, "Hold it! Now just hold it a minute! I know what you're going to say. You're going to tell me that I'll get a cookie and some juice if I put things away, but I don't want any cookie, and I don't want any juice, and I'm not putting anything away."

Once he was trying to paste a paper airplane together, but his dancing around interfered with his work, and someone persuaded him that THIS time he really DID need the proper facilities. George agreed on condition that the teacher remain out of sight during the process.

She did, but she was within earshot, and she heard him saying to himself, "Come on now, George; you can do better than that," and later on, "See, George, I knew you could do it if you tried hard enough."

There was the sound of flushing, and the teacher suggested that she enter the room then, but George said no, she couldn't, not yet anyway. She waited. There was a long pause, and George finally called out, "On second thought, maybe you'd better come in, because I can't get my pants up."

I've never met George, but I'm very fond of him. I think he's the type who'll go far. The young lady who told me about him probably feels that the farther he goes, the better she'll like him.

—katey

3 How delicate, how momentary

"You," I told our twelve-year-old, "have not been very good column material lately. Shape up."

I've been more interested in the blooms breaking through on the tulip and daffodil plants than in the children, and far more interested in the fact that I finally located the two missing cards from our best deck.

I found the five of spades under the upstairs telephone and the jack of diamonds under Amy's bed. And why should I remember which cards were missing when I can't remember things that are really important?

It's spring, that's why. When I ask a child, "Why did you use the lid of my cookie jar to give your duck a drink?" I am told, "It's spring, that's why."

Why is my little boy suddenly leaving my side to walk a block away to play with "that little girl" down the street? It's spring, that's why.

In spring, "a young man's fancy lightly turns," and my heart turns when I watch him grow smaller and smaller as he chomps briskly down the walk, arms swinging, little red overalls disappearing behind a newly green hedge.

He's three and a half and can't pronounce r's yet. "I will be vehwy ca'ful," he tells me. "I will look both ways, up and down the stweet. My fwend Bobby Shadow didn't look both ways, and he got wunned ovah."

Bobby Shadow is a figment of my son's imagination, and he got runned over because it's spring, that's why.

I have a little girl who went barefoot after school because it's spring, that's why, summer even, she told me. I went out that night, leaving Ross to baby-sit, and learned when I came home that she had gone to bed with those dirty feet.

"I forgot," said Ross. It's spring, that's why.

I sat, legs crossed on the porch floor in a shaft of sunlight. I just sat and looked at the tulips and quince buds and bees and leaf buds on the trees and the cat curling itself into a patch of sunlit leaves leftover from last fall.

I just sat that way, soaking things in, and people began to walk by and they stared at me as if they were wondering, "Why aren't you working? Why are you just sitting there?"

It's spring, that's why.

—**katey**

M EN probably haven't, but I have, lately.

Kids haven't either, but then, they're not old enough.

The reason the men and the kids haven't, and I have, can no doubt be traced back to self-interest. Men are interested in themselves, and women are interested in themselves, and kids are interesting. It never occurs to kids that there's anybody important around here except other kids.

What I have noticed lately, because I'm a woman, is a cluster of articles and comments everywhere I look, on the situation of U.S. women. Some call it a waste of talent or natural resources, and others merely argue about career versus marriage, a topic that is becoming rather dull.

It is somehow flattering to me when I see myself referred to as a "natural resource." I feel like oil gushing, or hot steel spouting, or as if I were being sawed off at the base while some distant voice hollers, "Timber!" It's a free feeling that can shift from the power of Niagara to a uranium atom, or any old atom, for that matter. Why be picky?

I begin to wonder about the rights of men when I read these articles. Men too are composed of atoms, and they too gush like oil wells, and they too spout and, too often, get sawed off.

I believe that men should be given the rights of women, if women persist in getting the rights of men. I believe men should be allowed to diaper their own babies without shame, to hang out the wash without embarrassment, to vacuum the downstairs, make the beds, and clean the kitchen without derision from their fellow men.

All these are exalted tasks, essential to the national welfare and to the proper use of our natural resources. A man should have the right to hang around his four-year-old son all day long, if only to hear him say, "The fairy godmother waved her hand, and a wagon came with horses, and the horses pulled Cinderella away to the ball game." (That's a direct quote from Ross's four-year-old son, and Ross didn't hear it. I did. I am privileged.)

A man should have the right to change beds and

cook and do the laundry. He should have a right to be there when his pre-teenager comes in from the school bus yelping because some undergrown male clobbered her with a snowball. He has a right to be caught by the blueness of her eyes as she tells her story and to wonder what he ever did to let the salty, ocean-blue waters flow so willingly and freely from her eyes.

He has a right to stay home on a winter morning and watch snowflakes drift and pile and cover until only a few leaves of the rhododendron glisten through. He has a right to make soup, from the initial boiling of the nourishing bones to the adding of the last finely cut vegetable or bit of spice.

He has a right to be warm, nourished, sheltered, and the right to be told, "Go out if you wish, if you must. I am here."

He has a right to all the daylong smells, sounds, and sights of home: water dripping from the rain spouting, beef stew cooking in the kitchen, children laughing in a snowball fight, logs crackling on the hearth, bird songs early when all the other people are gone from the house, trucks lumbering up and down the street, old boards creaking, the doorbell or phone ringing, machines of the house purring.

He has a right to see his own street, to see and hear autumn leaves plopping gently, one by one, like raindrops just letting go, or snow dropping suddenly from a maple limb, or to note, on the same maple, the telltale, tender shoots of spring.

He has a right to see cat or squirrel tracks in the snow outside the kitchen window, and to know the difference. He has a right to sing or even, as I sometimes do, play a piano in the morning sunlight.

He has a right to home.

And by the same reasoning, he has a right to keep it clean. Society shouldn't prevent him from keeping this lovely place clean. He ought to be allowed (he suffers so) to pick up a dust cloth, a cleanser, a bucket of water, a scrub brush, a broom, a clothespin, if he wants. After all, everything's so automatic in the home, and, bless man, he made it so. He made it automatic because he loves it and all it stands for.

Men love home and men love women, bless them. I think they deserve the same right to keep house.

—katey

A WEE brown sparrow, small enough to cup into my hand, trembled there on the spouting outside the window that I was cleaning.

I quit the cleaning long enough to look at his speckled feathers and at the wire-thin claws of the tiny legs that clung to the spouting.

"How delicate you are," I told the sparrow, "how tiny and intricate and delicate. How can you be such a nuisance when I could cup you, quivering bit of life that you are, in the palm of one hand?"

And then it flew away with its finely boned, feathered wings, and its hardly noticeable tail behind it, and it flew so fast that my poor, seeking eyes could hardly see it in its flying.

When I picked up the cleaning cloth again, I looked at my own hands and tried to understand the difference between claws and hands, between birds and human beings.

My four-year-old boy was perched on a physician's table, waiting for a shot, like a sparrow perched upon some stranger's rain spouting. My boy was scared, and because of that he talked flutteringly and distantly, trying to make me come to him and get him out of the thing he had to face.

I only listened. "Why can't people fly?" he asked.

"My hands can fly," and he waved them about, up and down and around his head. And then again, nearly bent with courage for the ordeal he had to face, he asked, "Why can't people fly?"

"Your mind can fly," I said, and I didn't go near him. "Birds can't think, but you can. You can think about birds, but birds can't think about you."

When the needle went plunging in, he giggled and kept talking, and he didn't cry. He felt very pleased that he hadn't cried. Afterwards, however, when we were going to the car, he held the spot where the needle had gone in, and he began to feel grievances against society.

He reminded me of all the things I had never done for him, and all the places I had never taken him to, and all the things I had never bought for him.

"You never buy me this," and "You never take me swimming," and "You never let me let John eat in my house," and so on, naming all the lovely things I had already done for him in the past and for which he was suddenly homesick because his behind was hurting so badly, all the things he "never" would have known about if I hadn't been there when he was feeling good.

I just kept driving the car and letting him complain in the back seat, because he was like most people who want to fly like a trembling bit of sparrow and get so angry when they can't, because he was so like people who want something and blame someone else when they can't get it, because he was clobbering my own life as much as the sparrow who clobbered at the rain spouting, because I couldn't think of a good excuse for "never" doing what my boy, the sparrow, and life seem to feel that I should do.

I looked at my hands on the wheel of the car and thought, "How delicate you are, how momentary."

—katey

SEVEN children slept in my house one night, six little girls and one wee boy. All of them had starlight in their eyes and tints of sunrise on their cheeks.

Some of the eyes were blue like the sky, and some were as brown as tree trunks, and some were gently between the blue and the brown, as if some greenery had blended itself into them.

Some had hair the color of goldenrod, and some the color of a blue moonlit night, and some had a mixture of sun and shadow in their hair.

Some of them had sudden, bright smiles that fell upon me like the sun coming out of a cloud, brilliant after a long rain. Some of them smiled as if they had brought their smiling from a hidden nook or cranny of their minds, from a secret, unvisited niche, like the shadowy, mysterious, flickering lights that fall upon a hearth when logs are burning in a fireplace.

And all the children were like the sunlit place that danced on my living-room rug one day, a flickering light full of the lingering wind-swept leaves of fall, brightness and shade mixed like starlight, moving, blending, sparkling, here and there and then suddenly gone, as childhood is suddenly gone.

I remember giving my children the last rays of an autumn sun to play in. They could blot out the fluttering shadows with their little legs and leap in and out of the starry sun-puddle on the living-room floor.

What a lovely, brief, inexpensive, priceless toy I gave them then!

Late sun, sky, shadows, and autumn leaves are toys for children, but I suffer for the children. I suffer because adult minds are toying with all these lovely things, forgetting the stars and sky in their own eyes, forgetting their own sunrise-pinked cheeks and the finely etched sunset lines of their faces that come like the grooves mankind has cut into the earth.

Ah, well, the earth has put up with us long and tenderly; it is vast and very absorbent. I trust the earth to the sky and trees in the children's eyes. And I trust my love for the children.

—katey

ONCE a little boy has scuffed off the toes of his brand-new school shoes, nothing you do can bring the shine back to them. I've tried. His way of life is there on the toes of his shoes, and the best polish and best intentions can't smooth away the lives and loves of a four-year-old boy's pair of shoes.

Now that the shoes are scuffed, how about his brain, if any? He has the shoes, and he has scuffed them. Does he have a soul, a mind, a being, and if so, has he, at the age of four, scuffed off the top of it?

If so, has he merely scraped away some excess shine to get down to brass tacks or has he permanently damaged a perfectly good surface gleam of a soul, and if so, what kind of polish do I use to mend his little ways in the world?

I like to think that his thoughts went along with his shoes as he chomped down the street, kicking through the fallen autumn leaves, stepping in and out of pools of late October sunshine, noting where the leaves dropped shadows here and there on the walk and seeing sudden little winds take the shadows off and go dancing, letting his new shoes and his new thoughts go with the October winds and the shadows, letting his little mind get scuffed a bit along with the toes of his shoes.

I like to think that while he was scuffing his shoes on his way to visit his grandmother down the street, he saw stones and pebbles and uneven places on the walk, that he found a puddle with the sky and trees mirrored in it, that he looked up and down and all around and got his whole soul scuffed beyond polishing.

I would like to think that he can shine without my adding any polish. I would like very much to let him alone, so that he can discover the bark of trees by himself, so that he can hear bird songs by himself, so that he can watch squirrels with nuts in their mouths, so that he can see for himself how the trees and street lights and rooftops react to October sunshine.

I polished his shoes tonight with the best kind of polish, and the toes are still scuffed. I have no desire to polish his soul, and no energy. This scuffed-up world is here, and he might as well go out and scrape himself on its shadows, its fading colors, its mystery of life.

Now, it's a small, tender boy I'm sending out with the scuffed shoes that I can't shine and the soul I can't fathom, but he might just as well go out in it as not. What else can he do but go out and scuff himself?

—katey

P₀₀R little boy. Here he is, a gentle creature of four and a half, with three verbose older sisters yammering at him night and day. Sometimes he sits turned sideways at the dinner table with his chin cupped in his hand and an expression of loathing on his fresh young face.

When I'm old, if I ever become old, how shall I recall his expression? How shall I dredge it out of the tired wrinkles of my brain and heart? How can I keep forever all the tense little momentary things? How can I capture a minute?

"I wish," he said with a sigh so long that it lasted his walk around the table to his daddy, "that I had ten brothers."

"I wish," I replied with a sigh of a similar length as

his, but without the energy to carry it around the table, "that I could accommodate you, little lad."

He and his sisters kept me hopping after dinner with homework, baths, hair to be curled, blouses to iron, dishes to wash, and the telephone to answer. During the process my boy Robby and I had a fight with each other.

He was trying to make his presence felt, and so was I. During our quarrel (and I was right about when he should go to bed, and he was wrong), I forgot all about the time he first saw tears in my eyes from peeling onions and, looking stricken at my plight, offered to get me a napkin.

I forgot about the time he asked me, out of the blue, after his aunt had undergone an operation, "How is Aunt Sara getting along? Is she all right?" I forgot that on Christmas Day he was longing to play his cousin's drums and then remembered that his cousin's baby sister was asleep upstairs and said, "No, I better not. The baby's sleeping."

I forgot too many of the events that are etched so minutely. I fought Robby all through the scrubbing of his teeth, and when I discovered that his blanket (he's another Linus) had been left downstairs, my rage spilled out too far over myself. I sent him scrambling for his blanket.

He made it to the landing of the stairway, while I stood glowering from a black railing above him. He stood there holding a toy bear the size of him, waiting for his father to fling him the blanket, and while he was waiting he looked up at me from way down there on the landing, and I looked down at him from way up there at the towering railing, and I felt smiles creeping into my eyes and at the corners of my mouth, and I loved the image and the temporary moment of him, and I winked down at my little boy, and grinned, and said to him, "Romeo, Romeo, wherefore art thou Romeo?"

He grinned, too. He knew what I had said.

—katey

Ross was working on his income-tax return, to which I have contributed nothing except a few additional figures and headaches, and I said, "How long did you say it was?"

"How long did I say what was?" he asked without looking up.

"How long did you say it took you to wake me up when Robby got croup last night?"

Ross looked up and out into the confines of space in our living room for a moment and then said, "Oh, about five minutes." Then he went back to the income tax.

What looks up must, of course, eventually look down again. What comes in must, naturally, go out again. What goes up comes down, and what comes down goes up, and if my boy came to me, he must go, like our love and our income, and I must say that it's quite a mixture of thinking I have going on in my mind right now.

I don't believe that it was five minutes. I'm not that inflexible. Anyway, once I heard Robby's coughing, I came awake or "to," if you prefer, in a hurry, and I gathered him into my arms and carried him to the bathroom, where I turned on the hot water of the shower.

Once it was steaming, I left him while I went downstairs to get some pills and medicine, and then, after shoving various things down his throat, I sat holding him for quite a while in the steam of the bathroom.

I wouldn't say it was five minutes, because it was

three in the morning and I'm hard to waken to reality. But it was long enough that I couldn't sit there holding him in my lap forever. So I put him down and cleaned the bathroom.

It sure needed it. If I hadn't taken the time that day to clean the living-room and dining-room rugs, I'd have found the energy and interest to clean that bathroom.

Robby, hoarse and wet with the steam, was bored with my activities. It was the middle of the night anyway.

"Hey, Mom," he squeaked at me from his croupy throat and tired little bones.

"We're staying here," I told him, and I think I was burrowing under the sink at the time, "until your voice sounds better, and if you like, you can help me clean the tub."

But his little eyes were too tired for all of that. And after a while (was it five minutes or centuries?) I guided him back to his bed. I didn't carry him; I guided him. He's only four and a half, and that's more than five minutes, or less. It's more or less.

It's enough to go on anyway, enough not to need carrying, enough to walk with your own strong legs. I ached to carry him. My arms and legs were full of an aching love, but I let him walk back to his bed and his stuffed dog and his favorite blanket, and the next day, at the doctor's office, I let him feel the sting of a penicillin needle without crying. I mean, he didn't cry.

He's the greatest little income-tax deduction that ever happened to Ross and me. And how long does it take to file a return? Five minutes? Ten? Eternity? You might as well ask how long it takes me to come down when I've been up, or go up once I've been down, to go out when I'm so accustomed to being in, or to be in when I've become so enchanted with being out.

Hey, Ross, lift your head from your income-tax returns and look for five minutes at your little boy.

—katey

I'M tired. There's a wee cold germ sneaking about at the back door of my nose, and I wonder how it found its way to the alleys of my mind. I never give anyone the key to the back door, but the germs get through in spite of my intentions.

These children of mine, who planted the germs there in my nose and probably planted more thoughts in my mind than I ever dreamed of having, go right on behaving as if I were not uncomfortable with what they have brought to me. They leap onto my back, make me swing them up and away into the air beyond themselves, make me draw pictures, sing songs, or dance with them.

"Mother, dance," one of them said. "I want my friend to see how you dance."

And at the dinner table, which should be a proper and dignified meeting ground, they have so much to say all at once that their minutes for speaking must be parceled out, and when that doesn't work, there has to be a game to see who can keep from laughing the longest. Whoever laughs first is out of the game. All too often Ross and I are eliminated first.

Oh, how angry and impatient I become sometimes, especially when they've planted a cold germ at my back door, and all their foot- and fingerprints and all their careless lives are scattered around through the house, and after I've picked up their scatterings I have my own mind to dust clean.

They grow so fast that I get annoyed with their clothing. They get so far beyond me that I think of them sometimes as I think of all people I've known, as shooting stars.

Long ago I remember thinking, "All lives are shooting stars. You can't tell where they begin or where they end. It is as if each life were shooting suddenly and brilliantly across the universe, and all you remember of them is that they were sudden and beautiful and fleeting, and that they left you with a painful desire to know more of their beauty."

But something is pounding the back door of my nose, and I'll have to answer it.

—**katey**

4 Closing the gap

THE following words are those Ross's daughters might say to him in the springtime:

I wanted to sing you a song I had heard, but you were talking about taxes and you couldn't hear me. And, as I recall, the last time you wanted to sing to me, I was talking about your rearing of children and I couldn't hear you.

I could become sad about this lack of communication between us, but for the coming of spring. You know what? I don't care a hang how you feel about taxes, as long as you're looking after them properly enough to enjoy my company later in the day.

You're terribly self-centered, you know, just like me. You keep thinking of your own day and what it has brought or hasn't brought to you, and I have to go through all kinds of shenanigans to make you know about mine. My day won't become interesting to you until many years have gone by and you're sitting about wondering what to do with yourself.

I'm loaded with dances and jokes and light-of-heartness, to put it the way people put it these days, and you don't catch on to me. Ah, me, the things I could tell you about the wee puddles of moonlight, and all about the patches of sunlight that dance on the living-room floor at the end of a day, and how they make me want to dance with them, even though I'm wearing out the rug.

I never told you how I love spring rains, walking through them without protection, walking through them with an umbrella over my head and listening to the drops, driving through them and hearing the windshield wiper swiping at them, or, especially and so fondly, sitting in front of the fireplace with the rain beating on the windows outside, where it can't get at me, and you can.

You're accustomed to spring. You've seen more of them than I. You've seen them from a vantage point that I've never had. Please don't take advantage of me. Spring is new to me. Raindrops are suddenly and beautifully new to me. Remember?

Love is new to me, too, like the raindrops. All that comes to me is fresh and new and exciting.

There's an odor about you that isn't springlike. You aren't a lilac. You're like an ancient maple tree or hemlock. Please be a hemlock to me in the spring. Or be the gnarled branches of an apple tree in bloom. Be the trunk of the tree, maple or hemlock or apple, but hold me, hold me, and keep my blossoms new, especially in the spring.

—katey

THERE's a new world dawning. I just saw my daughters dance. I was in the living room, late at night, relaxed, full of sentiment for the old days, humming "I wandered today to the hills, Maggie."

My daughters danced into my vision. They pranced before me, moved as nobody should. "We're starting a new craze," they told me. I know the box step; I was brought up on it. Only they did the box step in double-quick time.

Am I getting older, I asked myself, or are they faster than my times ever were? They box-stepped in double-quick time . . . but that wasn't all. They jumped about two paces to the left, to the right, to the front, to the back, faster than I ever could.

Uncontrolled, I said to myself. Wild, I muttered. What the heck is wrong with this generation, I murmured.

Where, oh, where, I said, did they get this frantic movement . . . notice, I said "movement"? I could have said far more uninhibited things.

"Daddy!" they cried, "watch this! A-onea, a-twoa, a-threea, a-foura." Oh, my, and my sore toe. Round and round they went, round and round, full of the movement, full of the spirit, full of whirling, twirling, swirling.

There's always a new world dawning. I know this sounds crazy, but I saw my daughters dancing, and it was new, fresh, like a flower blooming, like a person discovering himself, like shaking troubles and frustrations, like a world unfolding.

I was a very old person when my daughters danced. I hummed my old tune, before my daughters interrupted. I broke from my old tune reluctantly, like a person who feels bound to the familiar and afraid of the new . . . because it can hurt and introduce too unfamiliar and strange things to life.

Two girls danced, out of my time, out of my humor, out of my rhythm. I wasn't ready; I wasn't quite able to comprehend their style, their feeling for music, for dancing, and for themselves. (Don't all parents feel this? I hope so, because I don't want to feel alone.)

As they danced, moving so lightly and far more

freely than I would on any dance floor, I said to myself, "You old fool; this is how you'd have liked to have danced, freely, with grace (if you had any), and this is what is in your soul, your mind—what they have expressed."

Isn't this what all the older generation wanted, not just for themselves but for others? "There's a dance in the old dame yet."

I think, if I am frank with myself, that I'd like to dance as freely, as wonderfully, as gracefully, as unabashedly, through life as my daughters did that night.

—ross

ONE of my daughters had to write a paper on witchcraft. She waded through encyclopedias and dictionaries, and she talked the question around the family, and she finally wrote her paper.

One sentence in that paper that struck Ross and me was, "For some strange reason women were accused of witchcraft more often than men."

I wonder if a thirteen-year-old boy would make the same observation as a thirteen-year-old girl on any subject, not just witchcraft. "For some strange reason," she wrote, and I'd like to know what is really so strange about being a female. It's a man's world, of course. Everybody knows that, including Ross and even me.

Well, of course, consider the times that our daughter discussed. Those times came before women went jogging about the country hollering for women's votes and women's rights and all that.

Much of our history lies behind that bewildered sentence that my daughter wrote. Why should women, more than men, be accused of witchcraft? Why should they continue to be "mysterious" in the thoughts of men? Why should they, especially since females aren't really mysterious at all? They're just human beings, after all.

Shall I try to tell you why? Too much of the zest of living would shrivel away and be gone forever from us if little girls quit being different from little boys.

If my little girl's hands didn't send my thoughts flying like the wings of geese, and if my little boy's hand didn't feel like the rough and homey bark of a tree trunk, if she weren't there singing like the tops and leaves and brave shoots of the tree into the sky and wind, and if he weren't there playing about at the warm trunk and digging into the earth and singing up to the tops of his and her being, I would not much like being alive here on the earth.

He might resent her grace of being, however. She moves like the wild geese, and she is too often the colors of a wild, sweet sunset. She curves and sings and even lives like all the world, and he would so very much like to conquer the world. But there she is, shining like a star, too remote to conquer.

—katey

O NE day last week, I was asleep early in the morning and I heard—in my dim consciousness—a strange sound. It was a cross between a chicken's peep and a breathy "phew."

It was my six-year-old son. He had just learned to whistle. Since that moment of great discovery, every time he is in the vicinity, the faint sound of his struggling whistle comes to us . . . upstairs, downstairs. It almost keeps time with his steps.

At noon, when he comes home for lunch, his whistle pops through the peanut-butter-and-jelly sandwich; it resounds from the bathroom as he washes the jelly from his chin; it is his fond farewell as he hustles off to school.

At dinner time he brings his little whistle to the table, gulps his food, and departs with his lips puckered. At night he wanders through the house "peeping" away. He punctuates the TV music with some of his own whistling brand, generally a monotone. His whistle fades as he climbs the stairs to bed, but in that stillness of his bedroom, just before he goes to sleep, I hear him give a few last experimental tweets to boost his confidence that in the morning he will awaken with whistle intact.

Boys are boys, I guess, whether they were boys forty years ago or now. I remember the day I learned to whistle (my children tell me I never learned), and I believe the rest of our family was driven crazy until I finally emitted a sound that slightly resembled a trill. While I was struggling, my father told me, "A whistle is a simple thing. You just pucker your lips . . . and blow." I blew and blew and blew.

Oh, the awful days that a boy spends before a whistle comes. Then the wonderful moment is there. It may be a peeping, uncertain sound that erupts, but, by jiminy, it's a whistle!

There are some precious moments in a boy's life. We forget them too soon. He may discover a secret place, a toad, a green snake, a shiny stone, the constellation of Orion, the wonderful tug of his first fish, a special hat, the sharp crack of bat against ball . . . and how to whistle.

Now he can whistle in the dark . . . and that's really something.

—**ross**

I saw my son skipping off to his first day of school the other day, and I got a quick, poignant flash of nostalgia. It was the way in which he flitted, lightheartedly, up the street, stopping to kneel for a moment before some interesting and distracting bit on the ground. Then off he went again, his lips puckered in a silent whistle. I wanted to join him.

"Come off it, old boy," I said to myself. "You never could whistle. And how would you explain your skipping down the street?"

That's it, isn't it? The uninhibited, raw days of youth are wonderful days—the days of wonder, questioning, awful mistakes, painful yearnings, and unapproachable ideals.

Yet with those years behind me, I can't be entirely uninhibited (no more dancing barefooted in the rain), question haphazardly (my trained mind tells me that there is an order to everything), wonder at the immensity of the universe (the immensity scares me more than I care to admit, and the older I get, the more infinitesimal I feel), yearn for the impossible (dreams are only dreams and they don't earn the bread for the family), and cherish ideals (they are the guideposts that are broken by errant accidents along the way).

But the young lad skipping down the street said to me, "Hah, old boy, you're not that old if you can see in me the urge and surge of youth."

I was betwixt and between. Here I am, buffeted by the reality of living and conditioned by the necessities of providing for my family, but still filled by the simple wonders that attract a child: why does an ugly larva turn into a beautiful butterfly; how does a bird fly home; why does grass turn green, brown, then green again; how does a smile become an international language; what's beyond the farthest star; how does a thought go from one person to another and spark the same feeling and quick comprehension; who am I and who are you and are we as unique as we think we are; why is sex so important; why are we so troubled when we want to be so happy; why do dogs turn around and around when they lie down; what is heaven like; and what is it about a parade and marching feet that stirs the blood?

Maybe, I say to myself, these haphazard, simple questions are a link between the skipping lad and me: they puzzle both of us. Maybe I'm not so old as I feel and he isn't so young as he thinks he is. Maybe the sight of him tightened the bonds among all of us.

The child seeks from ignorance; the adult seeks from knowledge. The child wants from faith; the adult wants from hope. The child grows with no thought of tragedy; the adult grows from the impact of tragedy.

Don't we all feel this way sometimes, as a child starts off to school? There is a haunting feeling within us that we are children, too, seeking, stopping for a moment to scan a new thing, puzzled by the swirl of private thoughts . . . yet we are a little too adult to say to ourselves, "Where am I going, and who am I?"

We'd rather smile at a child skipping.

—ross

It became apparent to our recent holiday visitors that Ross and I no longer have four children in the house, but two sets of them, the two teen-agers and the two little ones.

The teen-agers have lost interest in sled riding, but the little ones screech with delight when they ride down a hill on a sled, slip over the railroad tracks at the bottom, and come to a stop. Dragging the sled all the way to the top of the hill takes nothing from their energies, because of the anticipated thrill of sliding down again. Only the walking home, pulling the sled behind them, when the winter sun is slipping away behind the barren trees, brings fatigue to their small legs. They come home too tired to remove their wraps, and only after a long time of thawing out or after a hot supper do their spirits revive.

"I will not take them," said one of my older two. "I won't slide down a hill. I'm going to meet my friend downtown, and we're going to shop. No, I won't go sliding down a hill."

Only a year ago she was sliding down the same hill with the same screeches of pleasure. Only a year ago she went to the campus cow barns and "kicked the cows up" when it was time for milking. She came home all dirtied with hay and perspiration and soot from the road she walked. Only a year ago she kept bringing kittens into the house.

Now she and her sister walk together to the school bus with their hair smelling of the special spray that keeps the curl in line, and they go with their books and hairdos toward the bus, with their own tastes in fashions and with a new lilt in their steps, and they go away from me, looking as if whoever is on the bus would be rather pleased, on a cold winter morning, to see them coming.

When the summer comes again, only my two little ones will bring me bouquets of wilted dandelions or violets. The older two will come with fresh-faced young boys, and they will look to me as if the down of the dandelion seed were still clinging to their ears, as if they had come almost newly born from their mothers.

It's odd, isn't it, that my older two, the growing set, should refuse to slide down a hill with my little ones, and that I, so much older than all of them, should suddenly feel that if it's the last thing I do, I must go sliding down a windswept winter hill.

—katey

TEEN-AGE daughters are the most wonderful boon—

and most exasperating counselors—to a middle-aged father. They have more ideas, all of which are workable, and more enthusiasm for this crazy pattern of life than Einstein had theories. Most of all, they love their father with a fervid passion, but they also think that he is slightly old-fashioned, opinionated, set in his ways, unyielding, and tightfisted.

They are right. If he weren't all of these at one time or another during the day, he would be eating out of their hands and kowtowing to every irresistibly logical suggestion. He must tread his delicate way through their delightful mazes.

Therefore, I hereby commit to expectant fathers of forthcoming teen-agers my personal ten commandments for their parental self-preservation and self-respect:

1. Thou shalt keep thy mouth closed firmly when those young ones about you have opened theirs. (They already know what you are going to say.)

2. Thou shalt speak with great simplicity but with a profound air. (Sometimes you'll get away with the evident, and there is that precious area of agreement on the little things, you know.)

3. Thou shalt guard thy pocketbook as if it were thine only birthright. (The checkbook is a bottomless well, and your pen is the limitless faucet.)

4. Thou shalt devote all thine hours to the constant needs and whims of thy beloveds. (There is no end to errands, evaluations of boyfriends, scanning of school reports, gathering of quick tears, and comforting of fading dreams.)

5. Thou shalt be perceptive and speedy at dawn when various loved ones tend to their ablutions. (The bathroom, in the morning, is a gregarious meeting place, but not for dad. He must shave and bathe in between numerous and insistent visitations.)

6. Thou shalt keep an ever-ready ear for the supplications and pleadings of the needy. (Even if your opinionated mind is made up, you must exercise fairness, a rare flexibility midst the "stream of consciousness" that flows from heartbreak to red-hot anger, and a sturdy mind that encompasses all things at all times.)

7. Thou shalt bend thy will, like the wind, to the tender hopes of thy loved ones. (Where in the world can you meet so many wishes as in those of a teen-ager? A will o' the wisp is a sharp desire in their teeming lives.)

8. Thou shalt kindle the fires of courage in their hearts. (This one is easy, believe me. Courage, I understand, is learned from example, and who has more courage than a stalwart father of teen-agers? He has survived many battles and his wounds are abundant.)

9. Thou shalt keep an open mind at all times. (How can a father shut his mind? That's what I want to know. Teen-agers use your mind like Grand Central Station . . . and they tramp upon it heavily. Sometimes you can hide out in front of a television set and a football game.)

10. Thou shalt love thy teen-agers with all thy heart, all thy soul, and all thy mind. (Ah, now, where else is a love so easy? The sparkling eyes, dancing feet, and charming quirks fill your life with such lovely loves that your cup runneth over . . . that is, if your trembling hands don't drop it.)

—ross

To be what he is 5

I DON'T like to confess it, but Dick and Oscar aren't doing too well right now. Dick and Oscar are the two tiny green turtles that we bought for Robby. They've replaced the two named Rodgers and Hammerstein that we had long ago when our teen-aged daughters were much younger.

They're Robby's turtles, and being seven, Robby cares for them greatly. The very day after he came into possession of them, I heard him downstairs, early in the morning, reading to them. He was reading *Ertle the Turtle* by Dr. Seuss, a library book that he must return by today.

Some sophisticated teen-ager asked him how the turtles liked his story, and Robby innocently answered, "They didn't pay much attention."

He later asked, "Why don't they eat the turtle food, Mom?" and I told him that maybe they were eating when he wasn't looking, but I don't believe that. Robby, who has been sick and therefore at home lately, has watched all the places where the sun comes into the house and, knowing that little turtles like the sun, has shifted their quarters from one windowed patch to another, placing their bowl carefully into little shafts of sunlight.

If Dick and Oscar die, and they have a perfect right to do that any time they feel the necessity, I'll be blamed, and I shall not be able to counsel my son on the inevitability of death, nor upon the vastness of it, nor on how much he kills me in every day of his life.

Now, that wasn't a clear comment, that last one about how he kills me; I meant that in jest. He has given my life to me, just by being a little boy. I'd have much less reason, aside from my son, to keep on with the trying and the caring and the feeding of life.

I suppose that I'd rather not take the blame of anyone's death. And yet I feel blame, and it comes over my shoulders in sudden gusts of winter wind, and I grow suddenly cold. I think about lovely persons who are now gone from me, in the winter winds or falling leaves, and I shudder and become suddenly cold and silent.

There was a kindness and love in me that I could have spoken, by a gesture or a word. I could have hugged, briefly, some lost soul. I could have smiled, or kissed some cheek, some withered, woebegone cheek, or I could have spoken, in appropriate terms, to someone longing for discourse.

I can't handle turtles any better than I can handle my son, and when Dick and Oscar die, how shall I tell my wee son about death? How shall I explain even his birth? I can only love him and try to make him see himself and be what he is.

—katey

As a part of physical education at school, the children run races during recess. Our third-grade son told his father and me the other night that he never wins a race because one particular friend of his always beats him, if no one else does.

One day, according to our son, his friend George (I've changed his name because he's innocent) won the race differently.

"How do you mean?" I asked.

"He took a shortcut," said Robby.

While I was laughing my eyes into tears, Robby began a game of hide-and-seek with our dog, Sam. (I was laughing not because I approve of cheating in games or life but because most people cheat under cover; George, in his innocence, cheated in front of the teachers and his entire class. I could just imagine what he was thinking as he puffed his small frame across that shortcut, and I could hear myself cheering him on, "Good thinking, George!")

Sam doesn't know how to play hide-and-seek, and Robby began his instructions the wrong way around. Robby tried to hide from Sam instead of letting Sam hide from him. After many tries, Robby asked me to hold Sam in the kitchen while he went to hide.

I reminded Robby, however, that Sam can hear and smell better than people. "Sam can smell you out from a mile off," I said, as I thought to myself, "and so can I." I also told him that he'd have to be very quiet because of Sam's excellent hearing.

I squatted in the kitchen holding Sam's collar, and Robby ran noisily into the living room, where he did a loud fandango to throw Sam's ears off his sound, and then Robby became very quiet. I didn't know whether to yell "Ready or not," because I was afraid Robby would yell back.

To test Robby's subtlety I hollered, "Ready or not, we're coming!" and from the depths of the front hall closet I heard, in muffled tones, "Yep, I'm ready!" I released Sam and followed him as he bounded into the hall, stuck his nose into the partly open door of the closet, opened it, and leaped upon Robby.

That ended Sam's first lesson in the game of hide-and-seek and one of the most pleasurable moments of my life. Little boys and little dogs should last forever.

—katey

Ross had a deck of cards when he was lying alone in a hospital bed in Austria. He played solitaire for hours. He watched a single fly in its wanderings. He dealt with pain and loneliness by singing every song he knew and by playing solitaire. He never cheated when he played because he would have ruined his game.

A few days ago I taught Robby how to play solitaire, and he has been fascinated with it. I never thought an eight-year-old boy would like a card game so much. I told him that it's a frustrating game, that one seldom wins, that I played it off and on for more than two hours before I won.

Robby wanted to cheat, and then again, he didn't want to. He kept asking me, "Can't I put this card up here?" when he knew very well that he'd be cheating if he did.

"Why shouldn't I cheat?" he asked me.

"Because," I told him, "you'd cheat yourself. If there's one thing you don't want, it's getting cheated, and if you sneak around instead of hitting a problem head-on and taking the consequences, you'll suffer, or you'll make someone else suffer, and if someone else suffers because of you, you'll suffer more."

He still wanted to cheat at solitaire. He figured that he and the cards were the only losers. I said, "Those cards don't know what you're doing with them, but you know. Don't try to cheat inanimate objects."

Of course, cards can become animate to some people, just because they have fascinating designs and numbers on them, and different colors and values, and odds and things.

One can try to cheat with cards, and what does he have to lose if he does? He loses himself to fifty-two inanimate objects of varying numbers and colors, and after he has secretly cheated, he sits there knowing that he hasn't won a thing. The king of hearts won't smile and say, "You won." The queen of spades won't pin a secret medal on him and say, "You won by cheating, and no one will ever know."

How do you say, "Don't cheat, little boy, but be yourself?" to an eight-year-old who has just learned the frustration of playing a game of solitaire?

Be yourself, I told him. Learn the games, but play them as you are. If you lose, all right, you lose. And if you win, all right, you win. Either way, if you're honest, you'll know more about yourself if you try hard and don't cheat.

Ross, in that alien hospital bed, couldn't afford to cheat. He had to live, and he knew that life isn't worth much when it's cheated.

—katey

W HEN Conrad and Cooper sped into orbit for their eight-day stint in the wild black yonder, I couldn't get over the wonder of it all . . . and my eight-year-old son took the incident as casually as a bicycle ride down the street. While the splashdown was occurring, I was figuratively biting my fingernails and he was napping on the living-room sofa.

I tried to tell him. "Robby, you don't realize the wonderful age you're living in. Do you know that when I was young the airplane was a baby, computers weren't born yet, and a trip to the moon was a fancy of a comic-strip hero, Buck Rogers?

"Can you imagine," I said, "that my father and mother courted in a buggy, that they needed the moon to guide them down the road, and that the only flat tire a girl had to fear was a dull date?"

He couldn't imagine. The easy comforts of this age were too much with him. "Do you ever stop to think that our everyday existence depends upon electricity, that the stove, refrigerator, oil heater, lights, iron, dishwasher, clothes washer and dryer—and a thousand other little things—are run by electricity?"

"Yep," he said nonchalantly.

Then last night the lights on our block went out. We were without power of any kind.

"Whee, Daddy," said Robby, "it's like your good old days."

There was no television, no radio, nothing of today for my young lad, and I was amused. I told Robby that there was still plenty to do: he had a book to read by candlelight, a deck of cards if he wanted companionship, and his imagination—and, I added wryly, "That's how all your conveniences started in the first place, with imagination."

I wonder. Man has surrounded himself with millions of aids. We guided Conrad and Cooper back down to earth with split-second precision. Our electronic age has given us armchair manipulations that perhaps can even cure splitting headaches.

I'm happy to be living in this age . . . but. If man has found so much, has fulfilled so many of his dreams—even racing to the moon—why can't he apply his inventive genius to himself? Why can't he unearth the key to the simple wants, the ones he desires the most—love, happiness, faith, humility, and kindness?

As I followed Conrad and Cooper's trek around our

little world and marveled at the intricate mechanics
that kept them aloft, I wished for another marvel during
my lifetime, one that would give me the thrill of my
later years. I wished upon another star: that man would
find himself and create new wonders within his inner
spaces.

—ross

"W HAT, again?" my eight-year-old son asked me.
"My gosh, Mom, I've been taking baths for WEEKS!"

For a couple of years, since he announced his inde-
pendence about baths, he has bathed without my super-
vision. I heard from one of my agents, a daughter who
walked in on him a couple of times, that most of the
baths he takes consist of sitting in a tub of hot water
with a homemade boat until the water gets cool. Then
he gets out and dries himself. No soap, no washcloth.

Also having insisted that he can wash his own hair,
he came downstairs one evening with the top of his head
soaked and all the hair at the back of his neck completely dry. I let that go.

Taking his case into my own hands one night, I
chomped up to the bathroom in the mood of a woman
about to tackle spring housecleaning. He was extremely
modest before he got into the tub, and he carefully
wrapped a towel around himself afterwards. In the tub,
however, all modesty vanished in the brisk and concise
way with which I scrubbed the bejabers off him.

Why he loathes getting into a tub of hot water is
beyond me, because he always feels so good when he
gets out. Most people are that way at night, I suppose,
when they've come to the end of a long day. Morning
baths or showers are much more pleasant, but how
many small boys have time for them in the morning
before school?

One late afternoon before school started, my boy came into the house looking like a bum. I told him for heaven's sake to go upstairs and clean himself up before I got sick looking at him. He wouldn't go.

But there was in the house a young lady who's a friend of my two teen-agers, and she grabbed the boy by the arm, dragged him upstairs to the bathroom, drew a tub of hot water, and said, "Get in there and wash." He did.

He came downstairs shiny clean for supper. Then he went outside after supper and came back looking like a bum.

I should say, "What, again? You've been looking like a bum for YEARS!"

—katey

O UR nine-year-old son suddenly came across what Bertrand Russell once described as "the terror of cosmic loneliness."

I don't know quite how to explain it. It started with his asking, while he was working on his arithmetic, what the "last number" is. His father and I told him that there is no final number, that he could count forever and never come to a last number.

Then I tried to tell him that there was no "first number," either, because you can divide one into a half and the half into another half and go on halving forever, and that there were minus numbers, too, that came below what he calls "one" or the initial number.

I had him more confused than I was. I said that we use the words *beginning* and *end* because we live in a practical world, a three-dimensional world in which days come to beginnings and ends like school years, but that time has more to do with our lives than we think.

How does a child change in a month or a year? How does a person grow old? Why can't you see the aging when you live with someone day by day? Do the changes take place every second or every half a second?

I told him that you can't ask, "What came before time?" because, I said, "What does 'before' mean?" And then I said, "You can't ask, 'What's outside space?' because what does 'outside' mean?" He began to get terrorized by thinking about the universe and the idea that there was no beginning or end to anything.

It was close to his bedtime, and I didn't want any nine-year-old of mine to get nightmares over the universe. I said, "Some philosophers used to say that we couldn't prove that we even exist. How do you know, when a tree falls in a forest and no one is there to hear it, that it makes a noise?" That question set him to thinking about something close, but not too close, to the question of the origin of the universe, if the word *origin* has any meaning except in a small-world sense.

Then I told him that Descartes said, "I think, therefore I am."

"Robby," I added, "I don't understand what the man meant so exactly that I can explain it to you, because some thoughts people have are explainable to themselves but not to other people."

And finally I said, "For three-dimensional people like me, who sometimes find themselves in the fifth dimension and wonder why they're there, I've revised Descartes to: 'I think I am, I think I am, I think I am,' and I chug through life that way."

I'm not sure that Robby knows the story of the little train that kept saying, "I think I can, I think I can," and finally made it, but after the terror is over and he remembers Descartes, he might say to himself, "I think

I am, I think I am," and thereby reach the summit of the cosmic thoughts that leave him without a sense of gravity.

—katey

Family circles 6

SOME people abhor the advertising that goes on in our country. Other people say that it's necessary to our economy. I won't take sides in the argument because I haven't time.

All I can say is that I get better results from my own children if I think about my requests before I make them, and that's good advertising.

For instance, our dog, Sam, whom the children love, came home after escaping from the house and running about unleashed for an hour with the cops breathing down his neck, and he was all tired out and panting from his run and the bawling-out he got from his master, Ross. (I felt as sorry for that dog as I feel when a two-year-old spills tomato soup on a dining-room rug from a highchair, and mom gets mad because she's too tired to clean up tomato soup from her dining-room rug and she should have had enough sense not to feed the child tomato soup in the dining room in the first place.)

Instead of saying to one of the children, "Get the dog a drink of water," I said, "Please get that tired puppy a bowl of clean, fresh, cold water." Off they went for a bowl of water for the dog. I used adjectives to describe my state of mind and the dog's state of being, and I got results.

My mother worked on me in the same manner. Instead of saying, "Go wash the dishes," she said, in a pitiful tone that implied that we had somehow done her in during the day, "Would you mind putting those few dishes through the sink and suds?" Or she'd say, "Would you mind running those few things over the ironing board for me?"

If she had said, "Those few things that need ironing would smell very fine of starch and freshness if somebody would just run a hot iron over them," she'd have done even better. She did well enough, and she used what people abhor as advertising.

She made an ugly job look enticing. After all, advertisers sometimes do better with making children brush their teeth than parents do. (I'm kidding, really; children are so conditioned to advertising that parents have to keep telling them, regardless of the brand used.)

There's a point for advertising, however. We're in corn-on-the-cob season, and if I want one of my children to husk corn, I can say, "Go husk this," or I can say, "Here's a bagful of fresh sweet corn, and if you go outside into the clean, fresh air at the picnic table and take the outsides off this corn, you'll find sweet corn there, and when you bring it to me, I'll cook it and you'll eat it with melted butter and salt, and pepper, if you like, and we'll all sit around the table munching corn together and have a fine time at dinner."

So it doesn't work three times running. Advertising doesn't, either. As a mother, I feel like Madison Avenue. I have to be fresh and new and enticing. To heck with it. I don't get paid.

"Go clean the bathtub," say I, not, "Wouldn't that tub look appealing if you just sprinkled a little stardust cleanser in there and wiped it out and then felt the clean, fresh water, warm and comforting, and all those deodorant suds falling all over you?"

A little advertising is good, but these days children know when parents are fakes.

—katey

T HREE of my eleven quarts of home-canned tomatoes didn't seal properly. I did them over again, and still they wouldn't seal. I did them again, and then they sealed.

Meantime my son was making apple crisp, and I said I would have nothing to do with him. If he wanted to make apple crisp, he could read my recipe and make his own apple crisp, and if he cut himself peeling the apples, I would not rush him to the doctor to have stitches taken in whatever part of his anatomy he had sliced instead of the apples, and if he got my tart apples all bloody, I would lead him to the nearest mess of quicksand and throw him in.

He said I couldn't do that because I didn't know where there was any quicksand in the immediate vicinity, and he wouldn't give me his recipe for it. Then he asked me how to core an apple.

In order to avoid blood and quicksand, I began to peel apples, and I finally found a way in which he could do them without my assistance and without getting cut. Peeling and coring apples with a potato peeler takes more time, but the peeler is much safer for a ten-year-old.

He made such delicious apple crisp that he and a friend of his ate half of it before dinner, and then one of his sisters came in and polished off another bowlful, with great compliments to her brother for his good work, and by the time dinner was over, there was a spoonful left for Ross, who said it was delectable.

After dinner, I cleaned up the kitchen and stored my eleven quarts of sealed tomatoes away and wrote a column. Then Amy came downstairs with a friend who had planned to spend the night, and she asked me where my recipe for chocolate cake was located. I told her, and I added that I would have absolutely nothing to do with her if she planned to bake a cake at such a late hour.

"You're on your own!" I hollered toward the kitchen. "Don't ask me for a thing!"

She must have heard me, because it was her friend who yelled from the kitchen, "Mrs. Lehman, how many cups are there in a pound?"

"Two!" I yelled back.

And then Robby, the remarkable chef who had made such delicious apple crisp, said to me very thoughtfully, "Mom, that can't be."

"What can't be?"

"Two cups in a pound. After all, a cup of molten lava will weigh more than a cup of feathers."

And I hollered to the kitchen, "Amy, are you using any molten lava or feathers in that cake recipe?"

"What?"

Before replying I asked Robby, "Chicken feathers or duck?"

While Robby was thinking, Ross said, "Horsefeathers," but finally Robby said, "Duck."

But by that time I was ready to duck out of the whole situation, and I did. I didn't even wait to see how the cake turned out.

—katey

I'M not a good modern mother. When the kids draw something, I don't ask them sweetly, "Tell me about your picture, dear." Instead I holler, "HOW COME YOU

DREW ALL OVER MY BRAND-NEW STATIONERY WITHOUT ASKING?"

When the small boy drags a kitchenful of kids into my house behind my back and starts parceling out the bananas or plums or peaches that I just bought yesterday, or when he starts mixing up milk-and-chocolate drinks and slops up the kitchen counters and floors, and I have a head cold, I don't greet his darling little friends with, "May I help you, dearies?"

Oh, no, not me; I yell, "OUT! OUT, ALL OF YOU! GET OUT! AND TAKE YOUR CRUMMY JARS FULL OF BUGS WITH YOU!"

I'm supposed to keep a happy little home here, one that looks as if an interior decorator had been at large on the premises, one that looks like magazine ads.

No, I'm not. I'm supposed to mother all the kids that come under my elderly wing. I'm supposed to let them find nooks and crannies in this house because they can't find them anywhere else—you know, all those hidden places in a house where a child can go and make tents or miniature hide-outs.

I've ousted them rather often, or perhaps not often enough, from various crannies in my house, because they didn't behave well. But I can't keep them away. I've made mistakes, too, and I know it, and I'm not nearly so good as I'd like the children to be.

You know, that's what the whole so-called question of women's roles is about these days. Everyone in this nation wants kids to be better than their parents were, and women are supposed to make the difference.

I'm only one of those women, and I wouldn't have four kids if I hadn't wanted them. I wouldn't try to be an individual if I didn't feel so much about life, about being here on the earth. I think much about God and being, and every kid who comes near me knows that.

At the same time, I put up with no nonsense from

those earthly kids. I'm here, too, for some crazy reason or another, and I won't let them drown me out in their childish laments or baby cries. Anyone who moans too loudly is not a mature adult.

I sympathize with the cries of children, but I try hard to let their tears nourish their growth. I jump and act immediately when an infant cries, but I walk slowly and calmly toward a two-year-old who has fallen, and I speak quietly and lovingly to anything frantic in a three-year-old. With a child of four, I turn on a little quiet heat from my own personality, and when they reach the teen-aged level, I let them have it. I holler, "Get your books off the coffee table, and, for heaven's sake, stop smelling up this house with hair spray!"

I get along fine.

—**katey**

Hey, all you dads out there in that great family circle, did you ever sigh sadly and resignedly to yourself and say, "I've had it!"? Take courage, you brave, stout-hearted men, take courage.

"Daddy," says the young lad as I'm about to savor my after-dinner cigar and coffee, "what's beyond the stars?"

A few minutes later, "Daddy," says the young lady, "I'm going to a dance, and I need a pair of shoes—it's formal [she doesn't know the meaning of the word] and I need a new dress, and I know it's near Christmas, and I don't want to bother you, but I haven't talked to you about clothes for some time, and . . ."

"Daddy," says another daughter, "I'm in a heck of a turmoil. Studies. Studies. Studies. And I've got rehearsals every evening—well, almost every evening—for A Cappella, and [she's a perfectionist] I'm afraid I can't get everything into this wonderful, awful week. How do

you budget your time at the office and at home?" At
home?

"Daddy," comes a question from a too-near corner
of the couch, "what was twenty-five hundred years
ago?" She's doing homework on history. She continues,
"You know, dates are fascinating, but getting them in
order is difficult." Yes, darling, yes, getting anything in
order is difficult.

"Ross," says Katey, "do you have any more five-
cent stamps?" Thank goodness, she asks simple, direct
questions.

"Daddy, please build a fire. It's cold outside, and I
want to feel warm inside, even if it is."

Sammy, our dog, whines, goes to the door, gives me
a hurried look, whines again, and I get up, grab his
collar, and escort him to the outdoors. No sooner is the
door shut than I hear his sharp bark. Okay, Sammy, it's
cold outside.

"Daddy," the student of history asks, "how do you
say Lord Cornwallis ended his term of office?" I reply,
"You said it well, honey, just the way you said it."

"Ross," Katey chimes in, "you've got some Jewish
friends on your Christmas list. What do you say: 'Happy
Yom Kippur'?"

"Daddy," one daughter yells from the stairs,
"where is my luncheon money? You forgot to give it to
me yesterday." Another adds, "Me too, Dad, me too."

Then, as I try to finish my crossword puzzle—
relaxation, you know—there is this exchange between
mother and daughter about teen-age drivers, one in
particular, a fifteen-year-old who killed someone in a
joy ride . . . at least, I think that is what they were
talking about, and I couldn't help paying attention to
part of it since any daughter who drives a car is of
concern to a parent even if she isn't involved in an
accident.

"Where, oh, where," I ask my harried self, "can a man get a little solitude and peace around here? Can't I be by myself, with my thoughts and reading, for a little while?"

Then I look around my family circle. I see each one, busy, full of the quick business of living and involved with ideas and thoughts. I imagine myself alone by the fire, alone with my own little being and self-importance, alone and lonely.

I look up. Each one is drawing me into his own circle, his own precious moment of life, and I feel that the fullness of living, the great and little distractions that go with it, are worth the spilling over . . . and my cup is full.

So, dear dads, if you yell loudly enough, you'll get your pampering, but remember: a little loneliness is a good thing, but within that family circle there are too many loving questions and too much care to be lonely for long.

—ross

A LONG time ago, shortly after our first child was born, I wrote a column that began, "It takes having a daughter to appreciate being one." What I meant was, "For pete's sake, did I do all these things to MY mother?"

Our first child did more terrible things than the other three put together. Don't ever tell me that a boy is harder to bring up than a girl. Our boy is the youngest, and maybe I was broken in by then, but he was—and still is—far less trouble than his three older sisters.

That first one put a stone in her nose at the age of two, ran out in front of cars, had a speck removed from the pupil of her eye, broke her foot by jumping from a wall onto a concrete porch, and otherwise kept me hopping. At four she got smarter about cars. She ran out in front of them deliberately, not through innocence. She stripped herself and ran through people's back yards in an autumn rain at twilight, and she tied one of her friends to a chair in the friend's attic and left her there, and she took off with her two-year-old sister on excursions that filled me with terror until they were located, safe and sound.

Did I, I have wondered, put my own mother through all that? I can remember her sanding the dining-room and living-room floors in the first house Ross and I bought, helping me to buy furniture for it, still cooking Thanksgiving and Christmas dinners for a mob of people long after all were grown and were bringing home grandchildren, and performing countless other tasks that made my life pleasant.

The tables are turned now, and I suppose it's high time, but my appreciation of my own mother during holiday seasons sometimes is overshadowed by my aching back. My daughters, fairly well grown and competent now, are a great help, but occasionally the staggering of breakfasts and lunches during holidays gets me. One at a time they straggle in, each getting out of bed at a different hour, each wanting something different to eat, each leaving the droppings in the kitchen. I no sooner get the counters cleared than more dirty plates and crumbs appear.

One of my neighbors, having just experienced the same difficulties at Thanksgiving, suggested paper plates and cups for Christmas. Why didn't I think of that? Of course, I'll have to get a couple of new trash cans for Christmas, but it would be worth it.

If Christmas is anything like Thanksgiving, I won't get those two turtledoves, three French hens, five gold rings, and the partridge in a pear tree. I'll get one burned wrist, three burned knuckles, two banged shins, five black-and-blue marks, ten broken nails, and an urge to climb up a tree.

—**katey**

Most of my female relatives are in favor of the women's liberation movement, whatever it is. I keep saying that I really don't care one way or another how they manage with it.

This isn't altogether true, of course, because I'm glad that I am allowed to vote. Sometimes I even vote for someone my husband tells me not to vote for, but I'm always at the polls, where I check off people's names in the proper blocks, and then I go right back to what I was doing before I voted.

It doesn't seem to matter how I cast my vote. I'm still a glorified janitress, which is a better lot than being unglorified. The truth is that I enjoy my "rights" more than most women.

For instance, I'm my own boss. If I don't feel like dusting the mantel, it goes undusted. If anyone else feels like it, I say go to it. If I don't feel like cooking (I usually do, even though my artistry gets chewed up and washed down people's drains faster than I can cook it), I don't. I merely tell people to go find something in the refrigerator or pantry.

If I want to make a flower arrangement, I do so. If I don't feel like it, I don't. I once made one in the winter, simply by cutting some pieces of barberry hedge, along with the red berries, and took them to a sick friend in the hospital.

If I'm expecting an important telephone call, I'll race to the telephone, but if I'm not, I'll amble the long walk from the living room to the kitchen, and if the phone stops ringing, I don't care. As one of my neighbors said, "That telephone was put into my home for my convenience, not someone else's."

When my children were babies, I was also my own boss. I nursed all four of them, but I timed them so that they skipped the 2 a.m. feeding at about two or three months. In other words, I conned my babies into sleeping from 7 p.m. until 7 a.m., and I also conned them into getting housebroken at early ages, although a couple of them balked a bit and gave me some hard times.

Anyway, I'm my own boss, and I wouldn't be a man if I had to take up arms against a hostile nation, if I could get out of it. I believe I have it made as a wife and mother.

Even when my children are gone I'll have it made, because Ross will still be here and he's his own boss, and I never interfere except to help him, and he never interferes with me except to help me, regardless of what task we're engaged in, writing, entertaining, or otherwise.

I'm glad I'm a female. I get away with everything short of murder. And I murder gradually and with great subtlety.

—katey

7 Peace attend thee

Our house is silent tonight.

The kids have scattered to various summer encounters, and the sounds that accompany their movements around our home have given way to an almost haunting stillness. Now their presence is felt in their absence . . . if you know what I mean.

The first night that no child was here I felt the kind of relief that every parent recognizes, one that comes of a release from noise compounded upon noise. You know the situation: one voice adding to another and another and another until you get a chorus, an unsolicited cacophony.

However, the next evening my ears became anticipatory. I expected to hear one of my daughters clip-clopping downstairs in that familiar step, the heels of her slippers plopping heavily. Then as she comes into the living room she turns into a light-toed sprite, dancing across the room, twirling and swirling like a miniature ballerina. What a contrast, I say to myself . . . and then I realize that my anticipation is wishful thinking.

As I get up from my chair to go to the kitchen, I automatically inspect the table for empty plates and glasses my daughters have left behind. They remember the time for snacks but not the time to "read' up." The kitchen counters are clean, free of ketchup bottles, cheese, bread, butter, peanut butter, and sandwich meat. There's no one to clutter up the place.

There's another child who sings in the bathtub. You can tell the length of his bath by the continuous songs that emanate, songs originating from long days before he was born to those from the Beatles era. They are sung with such easy gusto that they blend with the other familiar noises of the house until we're almost, but not quite, unaware of the lilts flowing from upstairs.

When all the kids are home, there's also an impromptu harmony that starts among three of them in the living room, swings to the downstairs hall, then the kitchen, where suddenly the melodies become wild and spontaneous. Who begins the session depends upon the sudden mood of one or the other.

What strikes me most tonight is another kind of silence . . . the silence of order. The house is clean. A disorderly house speaks up, clear and trumpety, but tonight it whispers. There is no coat on the couch, no loafers or sneakers on the floor, no shirts or blouses on dining-room chairs, and even the bedrooms look sleeplessly quiet.

In a full house, especially among juvenile kings and queens, there are always discordance and harmony, lightness and tears, smiles and fears and problems. Parents move among these contrasts with the hope of sanity in their souls, but also with the feeling that here and now is a fruitful culmination of themselves. It is called love, I think.

Anyway, tonight the house is silent. Tomorrow, thank God, there will be noise and disorder.

—**ross**

I HAD what I considered an ingenious idea, but I carried it a bit further and realized that it wouldn't work.

We have three daughters who can argue about any given topic without budging from their original point of view, even though they make concessions now and then when a convincing point is made. They have been known to keep us up until two or three in the morning trying, in a purely friendly way, of course, to make us change our minds. We never do, of course. We just get so tired that the whole discussion is left dangling while we drag ourselves off to bed, and by morning nobody can remember what we were arguing about.

In all fairness, I should admit that they come by this love of debate honestly, because it occurs to me that Ross and I must be just as adamant as they are. Otherwise we'd occasionally give in and say, "You're absolutely right; thank you for putting me straight, and I promise to mend my ways in the future."

But each one is always trying to have the last word. That's where my brilliant idea comes in. I decided that the next time I wasn't getting anywhere with one of them, I'd just say, "Oh, zymurgy!" I could hardly wait until one of them came home and began debating so that I could holler, "Oh, zymurgy!"

When they asked what I meant, even though there's a minor risk that they wouldn't bother, I would say triumphantly, "It's the last word in the dictionary, and since I've just said it, I've had the last word."

When they asked what the word meant, and again there's the risk that they wouldn't, I could say smartly, "It's a branch of applied chemistry that deals with fermentation processes, and it's appropriate to this discussion, which has begun to ferment."

The problem is that our dictionary isn't up-to-date, and it's possible that the last word in the latest isn't *zymurgy* anymore. Besides, they're not above going to the inside of the back cover and reading me the final line there, "For a fuller explanation see 'Guide to Pronunciation,' 'Explanatory Notes,' 2," and then adding, "Nyah!" or something equally edifying.

I could hardly get the last word effectively by yelling "2!" because it isn't nearly so impressive as "zymurgy!" I give up.

—**katey**

W HEN I had my first child, a daughter, about thirty years ago, I wrote the line "It takes having a daughter to appreciate being one," and that's almost exactly what my second daughter told me when she visited with her six-months-old Katey.

"If I hadn't had Katey," she said, "I would never have appreciated all you did for us children when we were growing up." I told her that what I had done was my job, my duty, that it was nice to be appreciated for it, but if I hadn't done it, she might be singing another tune.

If she weren't still so starry-eyed, along with her husband, about her first baby, I'd have reminded her of all the mistakes I made in bringing up children, simply because no matter how conscientious a parent is, he or she can never anticipate all the things that might go wrong.

I sat there thinking, but not daring to say out loud, "When she's two, she'll put a stone up her nose or break her arm or both; you can never let a two-year-old out of your sight for a second. If you do, she'll stick fork tongs into an electrical outlet, and her hair will stand on end."

I could have added that when she's three, she'll talk so incessantly that you'll wish you had never been so thrilled with her first word. When she's four, she'll put snowballs into the neighbors' mailboxes, or maybe she'll strip off all her clothes in somebody's back yard and run around naked in the rain.

When she's five, she'll learn to whistle, and at first you'll be delighted, but after two days of constant whistling, you'll wish she'd learn another tune. Of course, she'll start thinking when she's five, too, and that will be lots of fun until you're besieged all day long with question after question.

And no matter how old she is, if she goes away for even one day, you'll miss her. You'll even miss her when she finally leaves home and has a family of her own. There are two ways of looking at motherhood: you can say that you'll never be rid of her; or you can say that no matter what happens, she'll always be with you.

—katey

THERE'S an old song that goes, "I get along without you very well . . . of course I do." The song is a lie, because the singer really can't get along very well without . . .

The reason I'm quoting the old song is that I must make a confession. You know about the bravado parents exhibit when their children leave the nest. "Now, without them underfoot," they say, "there'll be quiet around the house, no distractions while we're trying to do the Sunday crossword puzzle, and time to do what we want to do when we want to do it."

Of course we will. Well, I must confess, the silence around the house at times is deafening. I've become accustomed to their noise. I miss the cacophonous background . . . a voice shouting from upstairs, the banging of the piano in the den, and a huddle in the corner of the living room where an argument is brewing.

Sunday afternoons were the best and worst of times. Somehow the friends of our children had the same notion on that day, and the entire first floor of our house was strewn with kids. There were avid philosophical discussions on the staircase, a burning fudge party in the kitchen, a drawing session in the dining room, a lovers' quarrel on the porch ... and a continuous stream of visitations to Katey and me that required us to bounce our attention from one individual or group to another.

Then there was the gradual ebbing of our children's presence, bit by bit, from our house. And one voice, and another, faded from the familiar corners of our home, and there was that unnatural silence.

The experienced ones say that you get adjusted to the change. I know I will. I'll have to. But in the meantime there is the haunting memory of the full house, the raucous sounds, the quick rejoinders, the sudden bursts of laughter, and the pounding of feet on the stairs.

Yesterday, as I was beginning to feel sorry for myself, I woke to the sound of my son playing the piano. I came downstairs, and my daughter, home from her term break, was batting at the typewriter. A few minutes later my other daughter, her husband, and their dog came in.

The afternoon was a shambles. The typewriter sputtered spasmodically, conversation was rampant, and my Sunday crossword puzzle was interrupted frequently as one or the other distracted me with a question here and there. Finally a friend dropped in to see me. He was an Irish friend ... and an Irish song or two was the order of the day. In the kitchen our children started another melody. We joined them. And the day blossomed.

I guess I'll learn my lesson. There is never loneliness, even when your children leave. Somehow, when the silence is all too present, if you wait, the sounds of your loved ones will come to you again.

—ross

Mᴜᴄʜ of successful living lies in an earthy ability to let go rather than to hang on. I once dreamed that someone asked me what in the world would be most difficult for me to do, and I said, "Dying."

I wasn't with child at the time, or I wouldn't have said that. If I had been, I'd have said, "Giving birth to another human being." Most people don't think about newborn babies as human beings, but I do.

Many people don't set out deliberately to give birth. Children, by and large, appear as the result of some other emotion or action. I've thought much about that, since all of us became engaged in the "population explosion."

I never belonged to a planned-parenthood committee. I never paid much attention to what everyone else was doing. I merely held my breath and dived in, and I was lucky, four times, because I wanted to dive.

Nevertheless, when the first one was about to be born, I was scared silly. I kept thinking, "What if I should die during the process and never ever see the little one that came to life from me?" And I would think, "What if the wee one is born all crooked and unable to know me or its daddy or rain falling against a window and into the green grass of May? What if it never knows sun or shadow, or if it does, doesn't care?"

It was a terrifying risk. It really was. But I plunged, because I loved life too much to cling to it just for myself. I loved it enough to let go of it, now and then, to have children, and enough to know that they, too, would have to let go of it sooner or later.

I wasn't blind at all when I dreamed that someone asked me what would be hardest and I said, "Dying," and then, as an afterthought, "Birth."

I had the idea that they, my future wee ones, might like to know rain and windshield wipers, sun-slanted spring evenings, hot summer days, leaves turning in the fall, people turning gray and getting those attractive wrinkled lines at the corners of their ancient eyes. It is better, I thought, to have lived and suffered and then died, than never to have lived at all.

Besides, so many lovely people before me had accomplished birth, and so many more had realized dying. If they can, I can. And if they can, and I can, so can my children. You know what I really think? I think if you can teach a child how to live well, he'll take the dying better than I.

—katey

W HEN my children were young, I performed a nightly ritual for them. I rocked and sang them to sleep.

Somehow, without much planning, Katey would prepare the dinner, and either she or I would bathe the young ones, and then came the time for the rocker and songs by the crib.

I remember that it was a very pleasant experience for me . . . and, I hope, for the child. But I had not recalled the peculiar sensations that overwhelmed me as I held each of our babies in my arms—until recently.

My granddaughter Amy and her parents, Kassy and Bud, came to visit us recently. Amy is only six weeks old, and she gets a little "colicky" before bedtime. Since I'm an old hand at soothing with melody, I volunteered to practice my old-time trick of wooing the baby to sleep. I had almost forgotten some of the songs. But gradually they returned to memory.

I took Amy in my arms, put her little head on my shoulder, and broke into a waltz, "I'm Dancing with Tears in My Eyes," She didn't react very well, and her sobs increased. However, I'm a patient man. I tried "Carolina Moon," and the wee one seemed to like that one. I repeated a few choruses. Then I stumbled into "Don't Let Your Eyes Go Goo-Goo." That's a winner. I got bolder and warbled, "I Wonder Who's Kissing Her Now."

I introduced Amy to Eddie Cantor's old show-stopper, "Ida, Sweet as Apple Cider," Al Jolson's "April Showers," and nobody's favorite, "I'm Alone Because I Love You."

Suddenly, without warning, that distant feeling came back to me. I felt my throat tightening and tears forming in the edges of my eyes.

It was her tiny hands. They fluttered like butterfly wings on my neck. They graced me with their frailty, and I thought, "Here is this little tender mite, so helpless, so completely bound in my arms, and so dependent upon me to hold her lovingly and carefully."

And her breath touched me lightly. It told me of a new life, a beginning that will reach beyond me yet will keep within her a part of me, a heritage.

It was too much. My voice cracked, and it was difficult, at that moment, to sustain a melody.

I thought of Kassy, my daughter. I had once held her as nicely and sung to her, and now her child was nestled here. My arms tightened ever so slightly around Amy, and they told her that all was right in her little world because my love was surrounding her.

Come now, I told myself, pull yourself together and give her a good finale. And I could think of nothing better than "Sleep, my child, and peace attend thee, all through the night. Guardian angels God will lend thee, all through the night." She slept.

—**ross**

SEASONS

The most important things 1

Wıтн no sense of history, some people knock while others hug the next generation. They do it because it is somehow fashionable, from one generation to the next, to hug or to knock. When the so-called public gets tired of knocking, then the writers start to hug, and when hugging is out, they knock again.

Nobody has any steady opinion or method for evaluating any future generation, and I don't, either. I'm just a little tired of all the words. The only reason I don't become completely pooped by all that I've heard and read is that I've lived rather closely with the next generation, and I've discovered that the members thereof are people like me.

Besides, who is to say, nowadays, which generation is which? People live longer, and one decade melts into another. I could, for instance, give birth to a child within the next year, and how could I say from what generation it came? Was it a World War I child, just because its grandfather is still living and wore the uniform? It couldn't be a World War II child, just because its father wore the uniform.

Could it be a space-age child? Count down now,

Mom, one-two-three-four, and what shall you call number five? All the ages of people living together melt into each other like the seasons, and so do the so-called ages of mankind.

What people don't keep in mind is that "generations" are not the few quick years between the growth and death of one man. Not one man but many, of all ages, make the difference, and the difference is subtle and not too lasting, in the long run.

When I talk personally of the generation after me, I'm talking about my own kids, but the real generation is not my kids, because mine are spaced out within a nine-year span from the first to the hopeful last, and the last one might find himself in an entirely different world from the first. Science flies almost as fast as time these days.

It's conceivable that I could be a grandmother as well as a mother, and I suppose that has happened to many people. So what's the next generation? It's mingled like the minutes of living and like the seasons.

Talk of generations is primarily political now, according to what child was born when, and which generation we shall revere for what.

How shall I bridge the seasons, now that I've thought about that? How shall I tell my children that I'm "autumn," that they're "spring," and that their grandfather is "winter"? How can I, when time and space come together into a space-oriented world?

And how can I say anything, when a spring-child gives birth and an autumn-mother also gives birth, and the life span gets longer and prolongs the seasons? Seconds go into minutes, and minutes to hours, and hours linger long in the seasons, and the generations melt, young to old, into each other, and life is only one season in the history of mankind.

—katey

THE important things you do, the really important things, you do with the whole universe on top of you.

You have a baby, and you are lying there having it, and you don't have a thing to say about it. What happens to you is not a baby being born, not birth as you think of it afterwards, but the whole sweep and pain of the universe.

You have a lot to say afterwards, about when to burp it and what kind of religion to teach it and what clothes it will wear, but when it's born, it's a thing happening in the universe, and whatever force moves the universe is the force that gets on top of you and takes over, and you are drowned in it. You're all alone in it, and you haven't a thing to say.

When I was very young, I thought I would learn to play Beethoven's "Sonata Pathetique" so perfectly that people would stand up and cheer. I never did. It would have taken months of work and concentration, and in the end I would have been ashamed of the applause. It would have been dishonest to take bows merely for recording a piece of music that originated with Beethoven. And even he did not deserve the applause because I'm sure that the universe was on top of him when he wrote it, and he had nothing to say about it.

It gets to be next Christmas before you know it, or next Tuesday, or five minutes of twelve, and you have nothing to say about it.

There is a force that moves through men's lives, and it moves like the seasons and the sun and the wind, making pain now and peace then and a mixture in between. Each man's life has its own force moving it, and all the little lives are mixed with the big one of mankind, and the universe is on top of everything, with its main rhythm, its sweep, its force.

Each of us can decide one thing: whether to follow the main force or not, whether to get in the act or stay out of it, whether to let the universe get on top of us or hide in a corner. There are many corners, many escape hatches, for those who do not like to have the universe take over their lives.

But the important things we do, the really important things, are the things in which the universe has swept over us and had the final word.

—katey

W HEN I was a child, I looked at a falling leaf with wonder. Today I see the twirling leaf as a symbol.

As a young one, I was intrigued by the leaf. How did it cling so tenaciously to the twig? Then, at a specific time in the season, why did it change color, die, and drift to the ground? The season, the change, the whole rhythmic pattern was a challenge to my ignorance of the world and its mystique.

Today I am more knowledgeable but, perhaps, not much wiser. But deep within me there is a keener sense of the seasons. As I grow older, they grow in significance.

I could say lightly to myself that spring connotes youth, summer exemplifies the burning quickness and alertness of young maturity, fall typifies the aging of wood in one's soul and the fulfillment—with its beautiful coloration—of a lifetime, and winter casts the white, cold snow of aging over us.

This is what I thought today as I watched the falling leaf. Where am I, I pondered, in the whole spectrum of history? What am I in the billions of years that passed before me and will pass beyond me? Am I a falling leaf?

Of course I am. I am one of the billions of leaves that bud, spring with green, hold fast to the twig, color beautifully with the season, and then float gently with the world's winds to the eternal ground.

I no longer have the innocence and wonder of youth. I must question where I am in this precious moment of existence, and it frightens me at times—as if the wind that blows me now, and then loosens me from the bough, has some import I can't fathom.

But there is this strong impulse in me. Beauty. That's the core of my being. I look down my avenue, a cathedral of color, and it stirs my soul with a magnificent beauty that transcends all my doubts.

There is a pattern in life, from the tiny atom to the tremendous galaxy of stars beyond my reach. There is such a symphony in living, from a spoken word that touches the heartstrings of another, to the complex workings of a computer. There are the yearnings and stretchings of peoples, despite their conflicts, that combine all the movements of mankind since his dull awakening.

In my fall, in whatever coloration I display, I feel as if I'm part of an indescribable destiny. Somewhere, when my leaf has fallen, there may be the answer to the wind, the bough, and the tree.

But for now, for today, when the leaf is tender and only a moment spells the difference between the clinging and the falling, I can only reflect on one tenet. I love as I've never loved before, I see beauty as I've never seen before, I catch the whole world in my hands as I never have before, and there is a quiet wholeness in me that reaches toward the atom and to the stars.

—ross

SUNLIGHT flashed one February day upon the icicles, strong, thick, with lines that looked like the muscles of a young man's arm. They hung from the spouting on my house and from the branches of the trees I've nurtured.

And then, in the unexpected warmth of a winter month, they began to melt, falling drop by drop. Those too exposed to the sudden light fell quickly, and others, hidden by the eaves of my house, kept their secret places and melted, drop by drop, in driplets larger than my tears. They quit their dripping when the light had gone, and the cold of night froze them onto a pathway I had always taken, and the sum of their dripping made a pathway of ice upon which I could find no footing that was not precarious. Shall I, I asked myself, place ashes where they have iced my life, or shall I put salt to melt the places where I have walked?

Shall I melt them, all those who are small, through the salt tears that have yet to drop from my eyes? Or shall I let them grow, in winter as well as spring, and let them crash, icicles falling from my middle-aged spouting, and let the thoughts drop into minds that will eventually go back to the earth?

How can the roof of my mind protect the eaves that lie like shadows under the sun of my being? The best of my muscular icicles melt and drop into the earth again. Spring was always there, inside the icicles, like water saved for a thirsty tree, like ancient tears from wrinkled faces, muscular, tender, old, going back, drop by drop, from where they came.

How can I, with so many springs hidden under my tears, give back to those who come behind me a single drop of cool, clear water? How can I protect them with the ashes left from my being? How can I tell them, with a pureness of rain, my first awareness that my soul held spring?

They have made ice from my thoughts, and they have left me with dangerous footing.

—**katey**

SOME fond friend once gave me a poem that told me to chisel, carve, and file, "until thy vague dream imprint its smile upon the unyielding flint."

I tried to chisel, carve, and file for many years. To those who are older than I, my "many years" may look like little moments, like trying to carve a smile into a piece of stone.

There are ancient rocks on the earth already weathered and smoothed by flowing water. There are other rocks untouched by anything but rain. And there are pebbles washed by torrential floods, separated into intricate bits of sand, especially where the waters of the oceans are.

You find the weathered, smooth rocks at the bottoms of streams or rivers. You can find others at the tops of mountains, where water seldom touches them. Pebbles are numerous, of course, and so are grains of sand.

Shall I chisel a grain of sand? Shall I carve my life into a pebble? Shall I try my smile on an ancient rock that sits majestically upon a mountaintop, waiting for the rain?

It is people I am talking about. Which ones are the ancient, weathered rocks that lived in the flowing waters? Which are the rocks that haven't yet fallen from the mountaintops to feel something besides the rain, which is not so steady and wearing as the stream?

Which are the pebbles that little boys toss, pebbles so numerous that they can be tossed about willy-nilly? And if little boys toss pebbles, what do they do with sand? They make forts, of course, or castles, and then the sand is washed away, like all the little people who have ever lived upon our earth and have been washed away in mammoth tears.

Where shall I go, to chisel, carve, and file? And what is the vague dream I have for all those grains of sand, if I should choose the sand? Does my dream have a smile in it, even for the mountaintop rocks?

Just exactly who constitutes the unyielding flint? I? Or some other earthbound rock?

I've been warmed by ancient, weather-beaten rocks with sun coming from the lines of their foreheads. I've held, in the palm of my own lined hand, pebbles of people's hearts, and I never tossed them. The wind and waters of life took them from my palm.

I have sat upon the rocks that stand on mountains, and I have loved and left them there. I have played with sand, as I have played with the best that lies within the hearts of children, and I have let the children sift through my fingers, like the sand, and let my smile slip past them like a sunlit shadow.

Whoever tries to carve or file or chisel a dream into a smile must somehow become like a shadow, and a shadow is only a vague dream's reflection.

—**katey**

Today is my birthday, and I'm going to exact my full pound of wishes for my anniversary presents.

I won't ask for a token for every birthday candle on my cake, because my next year would be filled, each week, with a gift. However, as a man advances in age, there should be concessions to his fancy.

Here is a list that I hope will be fulfilled before next February shows its icy visage.

I want a succinct, intriguing book that explains the composite philosophies of the world and is so captivating that it will inspire philosophers to present to us laymen a comprehensive scan of man's thoughts.

And while we're on the subject of contrasts, I crave for the elimination of professional jargon and four-letter words. I'm overcome, sometimes, by the studied phraseology of some of my colleagues, and I had enough, during my Air Force stint in World War II, of latrine language to last me for my lifetime.

I want the good god Pan to tingle the feet and voices of our youth and goad them into singing and dancing in our streets . . . and I yearn for someone to place lightly the mantle of humor on their shoulders. (A coed and her boyfriend smiled spontaneously at me yesterday, and heaven dropped at my feet.)

Here's a difficult demand. I want the students of today to drop their suspicions that there is a clear dividing line between the elder and the younger, the teacher and the pupil, and to visualize knowledge as a continuing process in mankind, because maturity never ends . . . it's the beginning of another beginning.

I want open arms. I realize that when one without guile opens himself to the world, he offers his soul as a pin cushion. Yet the risk of being hurt is offset by the pleasure of being loved.

And speaking of pleasures, here are some personal gifts I would like to anticipate: the varied shadings on Mount Nittany as I drive to the office each morning, the lone hoot of an owl at night, the warming crackle of a fire on our hearth on a nippy winter evening, the giggling laughter of my daughters, the bathtub serenade of my son, the quiet moment of loneliness when the moment is too big and the voice too small, the silhouette of geese winging across the moon, the spilling of words—frantic and eager—from my children at a family reunion, the figures of a father and son ambling hand in hand down our street, the sudden bursting of spring colors and the fluttering, dipping, swooping of autumn leaves, the surges of love within me without thought or reason but encompassing and overwhelming, the fascination of inward and outward worlds where a tiny cell and a star are alike in their respective universes . . . and on and on, like life, when a second may explode into an eternity and years may frame a careful, precise picture of what I am and why.

These are my wishes for the next year and years to come. They expand within me as the universe is expanding . . . and I want them to be part of me forever and forever.

—ross

ALL you of little faith, all you who never believe, all you who have little habits that you can't get yourselves rid of, remember that this is the month of the leprechauns.

This is the so-called good old U.S.A., but the leprechauns are among us. They have a way of following anyone with a trace of Irish in him, and they will come into your crooked smiles, your frowns, your hearts, and your terrifying way of making yourself felt.

They'll be hiding under the hearth where you built the fire, and they'll be hovering over the mantle. They'll creep out from under your wall-to-wall carpeting, and they'll trip you right into a rainbow.

They're hanging on every tear you have to shed in March, and they'll be tickling your belly with every laugh you shake. They'll be there in your thoughts about your grass and flowers, and they'll come around, if your thoughts aren't proper, and persuade the crab grass to flourish when you aren't.

They're in every blustery snow-drop that whirls around the barren trees of March, and they'll be there in the sudden sunshine that comes after the snow-drops.

Snow, sun, cloud, wind, rain, the leprechauns are there, leaping out, from the toes of the trees to the tips of the branches. Every tiny twig of a tree holds a leprechaun just ready to plunge upon you.

Every bird nest was helped by a leprechaun. Every little thing that wanted to take wings and go away somewhere, anywhere, was helped by a leprechaun. Even the flight of the greatest mind into the universe was assisted by a leprechaun who sat in front of the big man's eyes and winked.

I wouldn't be at all surprised if he actually sat on the eyelash.

I merely wanted to warn all the good people. The leprechauns are here. They won't have their committee meeting until the seventeenth of March, but they've been sneakin' about in the meantime making preparations.

I met one of them, in person, I did, and no one will ever believe me, but I did. He said to me, "Everybody's good at Christmas, but nobody believes in anything after that, and here I am, with my rainbow and my pot of gold, and no one knows I'm really here."

He's here with me, and I believe him, because I really did see him. He is a bona fide leprechaun who came out of the sunlit shadows of my being.

—katey

W HAT's the most important thing in the world to you?

Maybe, with you, it's your dentures or something. Maybe it's your pet or your pet project. Maybe with me it's the sheer comfort of being loved and loving.

When a seven-year-old boy asks his mother, "What's the most important thing in the world to you?" I suppose the question is colored by feelings, and the answer might come out differently. Suppose a seventy-year-old man asked me the same question.

I've thought about that, and I think I'd answer the older man in the same way that I answered the boy:

"Life is." Then the little boy asks, "What comes after life?" and I tell him, "Love."

What's odd about it is that I knew my boy's questions and my answers, and then I asked Ross, who hadn't eavesdropped, "What's the most important thing in the world?"

"Life," he said immediately.

"What comes next?"

"Love," he answered.

"You peeked," I told him.

"I DID NOT PEEK!" he protested, and I grinned and said, "So all right awreddy, you didn't peek."

Kids always ask, "What comes after that?" and so Robby did, and all I could say was that nothing came after life and love because everything depended upon those two values, and therefore everything else, unclassified, came after.

Ross said that after life and love came the mind, brains, thought, whatever logic we could reap from life and love.

And then, believe it or not, I asked our fourteen-year-old, Kassy, "What's the most important thing in the world?"

"Life," she answered immediately.

"What comes next?"

"Love," she answered.

"You peeked," I told her.

"I DID NOT PEEK!" she was saying, as Ross asked her what came next.

"Thought," she said.

I shall not pursue the questions because it's quite obvious that human beings, having life, tend to believe that the nerves in their bodies transcend rocks, earth, and burning stars, and that life, because they have it and stones don't, is the most important thing in the world, and only their thoughts could make them say such things.

I forgot to turn my son's question back upon him. I'm afraid to ask him what's the most important thing in the world, because he might say, "Popsicles."

—**katey**

2 To find forever

I'M an ordinary man.

I don't mean to be facetious or pseudohumble. I'm ordinary because I don't have the magnificent touch of a philosopher or make the ever-reaching conclusions of a scientist.

That's why, when atheists say so definitely that "God is dead," I wish I had mental facilities in either science or philosophy.

What prompted me to ponder about the probability of God's death was that I went to church yesterday, on Easter Sunday, and if God is dead, there are many unbelievers.

As I sat in the pew with several members of my family, I looked around me. I looked at the faces of the worshippers, and the faces reflected all of the basic elements of godlike characters: sincerity, hope, faith, love . . . as if God were there among them, tapping lightly on their shoulders with the Spirit of Him.

Now, I can't attest that God is living. I have no proof, personal proof, such as a visitation, a voice in the night, or a quick, revealing dream. I haven't felt God stir within me, nor have I known what other persons have described as a poignant experience with the Spirit of God. There is no feeling that God has touched me with His hand. All I know about God is that the Bible shows me the most beautiful way of life I've ever known and that the people who have practiced this beautiful way are the ones who have given a precious meaning to life, my life and others'.

This, then, is what my average mind tells me. If God is dead, and my fellow churchgoers and I walked out of church into a barren nothingness of a world—one without those basic elements of hope, without a spirit of love and compassion, without a mantle of kindness, without that breadth of peace and quietude—then please, God, move over in your grave, because I am afraid, terribly afraid, of a world without You.

As I sat in church and listened to my rector, I was comforted by his words. "Platitudes and rationalizations," a critic may say. The "God is dead" crowd may proclaim that I go into church to dull my metaphysical senses and heighten my emotional being. "Go ahead," they might say, "and succor your ego. If you can't face the fact that God is dead, we'll be tolerant of your inability to face the real world of today, in all its cosmic loneliness."

Yes, they may be right. I am lonely. I cannot live without the hope that I (and I say "I" first), my family, my friends, and every other lonely person on this earth will have immortality. I want for myself, and for them, the tremendous beauty of life, the awful wonder of our universe, to continue, the thought-piled-upon-thought encyclopedia of our centuries to last and last and to provoke and provoke our souls.

Isn't it ironic? By saying that God is dead, man also says that he is dead. He destroys his own last vestige of himself. I can't do that. I'm not strong enough, sufficient enough, brave enough, to say that I am dead. Right now,

I can't conceive of a world where man is only of himself and lives and dies within himself, a lonely hermit, a pilgrim without a destiny.

I saw a man kneeling humbly—as I looked around me in church—praying not only for himself, I suspect, but for his fellow man. I can't imagine a world, at this moment when we need each other so greatly, where there is no benevolent blessing—of father upon child and priest upon believer.

Oh, I know, sometimes the mind says one thing and the heart another. "How," my mind nags me, "is there a God when he hasn't touched me or appeared to my conscious soul? Why is he so silent?"

"Be still, oh worrier," says my heart. "The goodness of people is the presence of God, and their good deeds may be God at work."

I can't answer either my mind or my heart . . . but I do know this: without God there is no hope or promise. Without God there is no continuity of that breath of life, love. Without God there is no real, driving purpose.

As I sat in church, I felt lonely, very lonely, for a moment. I looked around me again, scanned the faces of my friends, grasped for what I saw earlier, the beauties of love, compassion, faith, hope, peace, and serenity.

I came out of church on Easter Sunday, the day of glory and sprung desire, glanced at the bright sunshine and blue sky, noticed the pregnant buds on the trees, smiled at the warm greetings of my friends and at the eager eyes of my children, grasped their hands, and whispered to the universe, "Be there, dear God, be there."

—ross

Our oldest child was "confirmed" by the church on

Sunday. *Webster's* doesn't define the word to the total satisfaction of my feelings about it.

I was not at all sure, first of all, that a child slightly under twelve would understand what she was saying when she stated forthrightly, "I believe." She's a little unsteady and unsure, like the miniature maple seedling I've nourished for four years, first as a potted plant, then outdoors with stakes and protective mulch for the winter, then transplanted to a permanent spot.

The baby seedling shed its leaves, half a dozen of them, the first fall, grew cockily, and gave me the impression after two more summers that it was ready to take its permanent place in the world.

Last winter a rabbit cut it down to stick-size, and now it's struggling to survive. What's going on with its roots is a mystery, but on the outside, all it shows are two tiny red leaves, a half inch from the soil. I have left it so. Either it has it or it hasn't, and I have other things to do with my time, other places to parcel out my feelings and my energy.

So struggles the tender twelve-year-old with "I believe." Only a few small leaves indicate that the thought will survive. Sometimes I think too much is dependent upon the mysterious hidden roots. There are tears in the roots, as well as the sun of laughter. Our daughter told us that some of the confirmands had to be baptized first, and she asked us about when she was baptized.

I told her about my sister's born-sick child, who had no chance to live despite the knowledge and care given to him by his mother and father, who were both physicians. Knowing that anyone could baptize a child, my sister held her newborn son and, with the knowledge that he could die too soon, felt an urgent need to baptize him there and then. There was no water left in her bedside container, but tears were flowing from her eyes, and rather than trouble the nurses, she caught some of her tears in her fingertips, laid them gently on her baby's forehead, and solemnly stated, "I baptize thee—"

Afterwards she worried about whether tears counted in a baptism. Her child was not "acceptable." How about her tears for him? No?

I get weary, and I say of that struggling maple, either it has it or it hasn't, and I have other things to do with my time, other places to parcel out my feelings and my energy. I can't afford to get watered down by other people's tears.

My child is "confirmed," established, accepted, but even so, it's a long way from those few tiny leaves to eventual, firm-rooted bloom and belief.

—katey

I was wondering if evening grosbeaks can sail, if they can dip silently in and out of treetops without flapping their wings. Something quiet and yellow-breasted went winging between the budding treetops and the sky, sailing, sunlit, graceful, filling me with a longing to be more of spring than I am.

Yes, they can sail, the evening grosbeaks. I checked on them. Oh, my, how nicely they can sail! And how awkward I am, how big, how very unlovely, when I look at the budding treetops, at the grosbeaks winging, at the delicately tinted early tulips rising out of the earth in my flower bed.

How well the birds sing. How silently and beautifully the flowers bloom. How quiet the moon, how warm the sun, how gentle the rain that falls upon the earth in the springtime. How green and quick and unquestioning, how automatic and beautifully dependable is spring.

And how good it smells! I look, all around me, and

I think it's a poignant shame about us people. In a strange, mysterious way, it's a crying shame.

It's a shame that *forever* has such a haunting meaning for us. We made the word *forever*, and we live with it. We haven't told the birds or the tulips or the sun or the earth. We told ourselves the word, and we live with it, living too hard to be springtime.

"Forever," we say, as we look at the evening grosbeaks, hear the wind, feel the rain, or pluck weeds from our flower beds. Forever the stars, the earth, the rocks, the lichen, the water . . . forever the life, going and coming, like night and day, like ebbing and flowing. Bones and ashes, forever, petals and stones, forever after, minds and birds' wings, forever and forever and ever after.

It's a crying, poignant shame, in the springtime.

—katey

T HE other day when the thunder cracked and our shivering dog tried to climb into the refrigerator for shelter, I thought of the quality of fear in man, the sheer fright that leads him to do even stranger things. It isn't so easy to describe as Sewell did: "Fear is the tax that conscience pays to guilt," or as Shakespeare wrote: "Present fears are less than horrible imaginings."

I remember during World War II when I was a bombardier-navigator on a Flying Fortress bomber, the flak from enemy guns blanketed us on our first mission. I was so frightened that my shoulders hunched up to my flak helmet and, when the first German fighters came into my gunsight, I fired instead at the ground, twenty-five thousand feet below.

Then there was our waist gunner, who stuttered. When he came on the intercom to announce enemy fighters to our right, there wasn't a trace of a stutter.

We learned that the man who said he felt no fear during combat was either a fool or a madman. As our missions increased, we lived with our fear—it squeezed out of our pores—but we also learned to perform our stark duties capably with fear leaning on our backs. On that first mission, we could have been like dogs trying to climb into some refrigerator, but a conditioned mind pushes fear to the rims of a man's soul.

War, however, is not the ultimate in fear. With me it wasn't. Fear comes unexpectedly, in simple places and simple circumstances. I believe my most terrifying moment occurred when I took Katey to the hospital for the birth of our first child. There in the hospital corridor, as Katey lay in the labor room, I experienced the most terrible, lonely moments that ever hit me.

But fear isn't confined to matters of life or death. It can creep into a casual conversation, such as one that happened in my office last year. A student and I were talking about the strained relationships between various factions on campus. In the middle of our conversation, he said, "I am a student, and I'm for students." I replied, "I am a man, and I'm for mankind." He smiled derisively and uttered one obscenity, calmly and carefully. Fear struck me then, quickly. "How do I reach you?" I thought. "How do I reach out my hand and my mind?"

I thought then of a two-line poem by Edwin Markham:

He drew a circle and left me out.
I drew a circle and brought him in.

There is one comfort that man cannot share with that poor dog of mine. We can think and rationalize. For most fears we can seek such antidotes as hope, love, faith, and compassion. We can comfort each other and reach out our hands and minds.

At least it works for me. There is tender concern waiting at the edge of the circle, if we only sense it and emerge from the cocoon fear weaves.

—ross

"WHAT's the business, that such a hideous trumpet calls to parley the sleepers of the house?"

That's a question popped by Lady MacBeth in a play by Shakespeare. I could pop the same question any morning of the week.

Early in the morning a small boy trumpets into our bedroom, chomps all the way around the bed until he comes to where I am sleeping, hammers on my shoulder, and I could rouse myself with "What's the business?" but I know full well why the little man has called to parley the sleepers of the house. Routine business, but essential, is worth the alternative to not being parleyed.

'Tis better to be parleyed early than not to be parleyed at all.

I mention this because I met an engineering graduate of Penn State who said, first, "Study of English composition is a waste of time," and, second, "When they taught me what I needed to know to write a good report, it was fine, but when they went into *Macbeth*, they were silly. Who needs it? I just haven't used it."

I'm sorry to hear that he hasn't been able to "use" it. Sometimes, when my nails are full of garden dirt or stains from berries that I've made into jam, I quote Lady Macbeth: "What, will these hands ne'er be clean?"

And sometimes, when I hear, know, or read about a retired man who has accomplished something worthy of award from his fellow men, I say to myself, "Well, now, who would have thought the old man to have had so much blood in him?"

These bits are from *Macbeth*, from Shakespeare, but, as the man said, "Who needs him?"

My young sister had a little boy who died at the age of eight months, brown curls and all, and not long after he was buried, my sister and I saw *Hamlet* together. When the show was over, my sister, pregnant with her second child, fresh from the funeral of her first, said quietly to me, "Good night, sweet prince, and flights of angels sing thee to thy rest."

That, too, was Shakespeare, but as the man said, who needs him?

My sister is dead now, too, and sometimes I think, when I am in a crowd of people, "Bear with me; my heart is in the coffin there with her, and I must pause till it come back to me."

That's Shakespeare, but who needs him?

And Shakespeare said, "O judgment! thou art fled to brutish beasts, and men have lost their reason."

Who needs him?

—**katey**

T HE other night Katey called me from my casual viewing of a television program into the fragrant night. It was a rare and beautiful evening.

The odor of fading lilacs greeted me, and the budding leaves of our trees spread daintily through the light of the full moon. Suddenly a line from my past came to me, and I muttered to myself, "The moon was a ghostly galleon tossed upon cloudy seas." An eerie mood struck me.

The fragrance and the still night captured a similar night many years ago when I was a youth. I was restless; I felt a deep yearning within me, half searching, half melancholy. And I went out to the moon and stars, and I sat in the wet grass.

What is there in us that cries out? Is it the wonder of the universe that bewilders, the hidden emotions and thoughts that seek the artist's canvas, the yen for a quiet perspective and a peace that soothes a disturbing mystery, or a reaching for a love that isn't within reach? Or is there, in youth and in any age, a gnawing within our souls, a half glimpse at beauties and frustrations, and the intermingling of these conglomerates that propels us suddenly onto the grass under the moon?

I remember that night. I sat under a tree. I traced the fingerling branches to the moon. I looked at the stars on the horizon and was awed by the infinite distance between me and the winking canopy. I was frightened and fascinated.

And it came to me, the disquieting moment. "Thoughts are like the universe," I said to myself. "There is no beginning, no end to a thought. It begins where and ends where . . . in the mind of God, in the explosion of a star or a universe, or in the mud where an amoeba framed a man?"

Under the moon, I thought I could piece together my own being, place the jigsaw puzzle of my thoughts, emotions, and motives into a coherent pattern . . . but I discovered that the quiet of an evening may only invite the exploration of the perplexity of my existence. Exquisite beauty may flood the soul, but it may also flood the mind.

In retrospect, now, I find that I still want to sit under the moon. I still want to delve into the mysteries that frighten and fascinate me. I still yearn for answers that I probably will never reach.

Yet, there is one clear meaning that sings to me, when I reach for the moon. I see beauties with patterns that are endless, I hear voices that ring my soul, I touch haunting thoughts that tantalize my mind, and I feel love that glows within my universe as brightly as Venus.

—**ross**

Night cannot meet day head-on, in a clash. There must be a blending between them, because the one is the other, even if it appears to us that they are different.

If night ever met day, the twenty-four-hour period would have to bend in the middle, and it would surely crack in two.

There are really no opposites. Left is of the same substance as right, and right of the same as wrong. Day is composed of night, and night of day. Love is on a curve that belongs to hate on the other side of it, and there can't be any separation between them without chaos, and they can't come together without cracking in two.

They round about and into each other, all that we call opposites. One cannot exist without the other, and the secret blending between them gives them the same substance. Blending and shifting, they form a unit, whole, miraculously complete.

Try to find the dividing line, sharp and clear, between light and dark, sunrise and high noon, sunset and midnight, midnight and noon, love for mankind and hate for it. There is no line between these, but only an intricate blending that flows like music from one to the other and makes, finally, all one note.

Whatever the universe is, it is whole, not this or that, not dark versus day, but a thing connected and blended by secret lines, like the fine lines that come to people's faces when they grow older. What day, what time, was it, when the lines began to come?

What time is it, or is it all the same time? Am I as close to time as the trees and the earth? What is the time that hovers between life and death? Or is it not time at all, but a mysterious blending, that makes life circle around toward death, as light, casting telltale shadows, comes around to dark, and dark, tormented by shafts of unexpected light, goes around to noon?

Whatever blends our so-called opposites makes them all of the same.

—katey

You may, if you care to, put your burial wishes into your will, but the chances are that you'll be long buried before anyone knows what those wishes were. That's because people usually bury their loved ones before they read the will.

I learned that the other day when Ross and I updated our wills. Nobody likes to make wills—nobody except an aunt of mine who kept threatening to change hers every time a relative crossed her. Sometimes I think my aunt spent more hours changing her will around than she did teaching, but that isn't fair of me.

No one likes to discuss wills, especially Ross. And I, too, find it rather boring. What do I have that anyone would want after I'm dead? After all, I'm the important creature in their lives, and I've accumulated nothing materially that they'd want, not even a keepsake. Besides, after I'm gone, I won't be around to care.

But that's selfish. When I was in Philadelphia taking care of my granddaughter, my daughter and her husband asked me, when the subject happened by, what they should do with my "remains," and I said, "Cremate me and scatter my ashes on the top of Tussey Mountain, near Little Flat Tower, where the laurel grows."

When I told Ross about Tussey Mountain, he said he preferred Mount Nittany, which, I told him, meant more to him than to me because I was brought up here and knew a little more about the mountains. As Ross puts it, we "compromised," and he decided on Tussey. May the laurel grow; I hope we don't deprive it; may earthquakes cease and desist in that place.

I love old graveyards, and I think they should be preserved. There was one in Lancaster next to a church that I liked to pass when I went walking. And one time, just after I had given birth to our first child, a graveyard salesman came by to sell me a couple of lots. My mind was on birth then, not death, although death-thoughts had crept into my mind all during my pregnancy. But because we were transient, not knowing how long Ross would stay in Lancaster, I turned down the salesman, gently.

I do know that it's important to some family members to go visit graves; I myself felt a kind of strange peace after visiting my sister's grave more than a year after she died, even though I had never seen it before and probably never will again.

I also stood on a hilltop where my grandmother, grandfather, two of their children whom I had never known, and my aunt were buried. I felt haunted by their presences there, in the sense that one becomes haunted by a fragrance of someone missing, or by walking a path that someone you loved once walked.

I have no wish to deprive my heirs of putting flowers on my grave, and I don't want to spoil any spot that they might visit if all they can think about it is that my ashes are there. I feel like a quick thought in the universe, and if there's nothing left for remembrance, then I was just as important as the bloom of a laurel on a mountaintop.

—katey

Between earth and sky 3

ONCE, when she was trying to describe her love of the West, Agnes DeMille wrote a long sentence, and from that sentence I remember these words: "earth and sky clash."

I am not from the West, but I have been there, and I have seen how earth and sky clash, and I have been overpowered by the seeing. The West is home to Agnes DeMille, and I have longed for an understanding of how it must be to grow up in a place where earth and sky clash.

One short, breathless glimpse is all I have known of it. I was not there long enough to make it a part of myself. I was there only long enough to catch my breath and then look around helplessly for little places to go in all that sweep of earth and sky.

I was born in Pennsylvania, among the little green sheltered hills that are not home to Agnes DeMille. There are places I know in the hills of Centre County, places where only a little sky comes through at the tops of the hemlocks.

There is much earth in these places, but very little sky, just enough for the sunlight to make patterns on the moss and stones and to ripple through the waters that tumble quietly down a mountainside.

I have lived in a place of meticulous detail, with no earthshaking clashes. I have learned to walk through these woods with my head down so that I might know where my feet are treading.

Rocks, toads, tree roots, or snakes could trip me up if my eyes were skyward as I walked. Even if I looked upward, the sky would be designed by the delicate interlacing of oak leaves and pine needles. The sky would not clash with where I walked; there would be a careful connection between earth and sky. A tree would begin under the ground where I walked and blend upward with my vision of the sky.

If I walked without looking down, I would miss the tiny red lichen, no less red than a western sunset because it is little. I would miss the cool toadstools, the moist white Indian pipes, the teaberries hidden under their leaves, the sheen on rhododendron leaves that dip downward towards the streams. I would miss the clarity of water that rolls over the rounded rocks in those streams.

I would miss the daddy-longlegs, the cool grace of trout, the fragrant pink arbutus that trails along so close to the ground. I would miss the difference between laurel in bloom and sunlit, laurel leaves bending gracefully to drops of rain falling upon them, and laurel poking up out of the snow. I would miss all the triumphant green things that push themselves through the snow.

Thus it is that women born in the sequestered mountains sit with their arms bent and folded across their knees, and women born in the West silhouette their outstretched arms against the horizon.

—katey

A THOUGHT is the most beautiful element in this wonderful, cockeyed universe.

Yesterday I was pondering over this seemingly simple, spontaneous action of the mind, because I suddenly touched Katey and said, "You're graceful."

How many billions of years did it take me to come to that conclusion and that specific thought? When did the mechanism in a simple amoeba begin adjusting to a metaphysical spark? How did that beautiful spark find a home, find positive and negative responses, and then begin that tenuous network of reaction and counteraction?

Was it Descartes who said, "I think, therefore, I am"? It might have been Descartes—or at least his disciples—who made me start pacing around the dining room table one night when I was about twelve years of age. I was frightened. I suddenly discovered that I was a centrum of thought, that I was I, and the consciousness of being I and no one else was too much for me. I felt at one moment like a god—because I was a unique, concentric person—and yet so, so frail, because I was alone with myself and my forming thoughts.

Now that I am older and know that I am frail and full of many doubting and fulfilling thoughts, I am clinging eagerly to thoughts. They are my lifelines to beauty, to conscious deeds, even to the tragedies that I now know I must suffer. Yet life is a precious, poignant episode for me, the only episode in these billions of years that has clear meaning and impact to me . . . the I.

I am a sentimentalist. I can attach great significance to the "pure thought," the one that springs from logic and order, the one that prompts great minds to formulate cohesive patterns for mankind. However, it is in the soul of me—and I don't know if it evolves from a religious or a cosmic sense—that a thought sings like a mourning dove in the quiet morning.

I only know that it is so precious to be alive, to think darkly and sweetly, to look at a falling star and wonder, to grasp at a curtain of the mind and peer into the unknown, to sit with a book and visit with great and ordinary men, to sit with a friend and explore our senses and sensitivities, to savor the fullness and query the fragments of all the universe that have entered and touched me.

Today I look through my window, see the sunlight dappling the trees and casting gentle shadows on the green, and I draw a deep breath, throw one big thought to the far reaches of the universe, and say, "I think. I live. I love. I'm grateful."

—ross

W HY should I suddenly think of all the soft things I've known? There was once a crying baby in a crib, and the darkness of the room there was as soft as the crying, and so was the little head I stroked back into sleep, and so was the sleep.

The wee head felt like the down off a newborn duckling, and the night's shadows fell softly on my own head, and after the wee one was taken quietly into sleep, my own thoughts came softly, like the sifting of flour for a light cake, like sand falling between my fingers.

I have a minute hourglass. The sand falls from one bulb to another in a minute. The sand falls softly, and the egg that my boy times, by turning the bulb four times, boils quietly, and my son's thoughts, as he watches the sand tumbling, tumble softly.

I don't know what his thoughts are as he watches, but they aren't loud, cacophonous thoughts. They are quiet as the flutter of a butterfly's wings, quiet as the blue of his eyes or the flick of his eyelids. He sits silently, watching the sand fall, putting his little thoughts into falling sand where there can be no imprint of his thinking.

Feathers are soft and, sometimes, so are memories. I remember a feather bed and a softhearted grandmother and the soft bed that she gave me to sleep in.

Puppies, kittens, and little lambs are soft. So are the thoughts of children. And so, too, are buds that bloom in the springtime. The buds of cherry and quince come forth softly and quietly like the tulips. Rain, too, after its thunder, often falls softly upon the grass and the flowers and people's souls, like the aftermath of pain, and then lets go quietly on windows.

Soft is the touch you put upon someone you love, and softly eager the response.

Winds whistle softly through the tops of trees in the summer. Sun falls softly in the summer, dappling forests and roads, touching, oh, so quietly, whatever human being wants to be touched quietly by sunlight.

And the light of a summer moon is even softer than the sun. Taking the warmth of the sun, the moon shines softly on quivering leaves, on laps of water seeking the shore, on wet pebbles, on anything that will give back the shine, even the minds of little people.

There is a soft core within all of us, without which the hard core would not be possible.

—katey

P AST poets, at least those in my own small past, have deplored the "masks" people wear in their being with each other.

A hat, a smile where no smile is, a look that says one thing while the heart feels another, a statement placidly uttered from a mind a thousand miles away from the statement, a formal handshake from sensitive fingers that might prefer less formality but never dare, a proper tie, a well-creased pair of trousers, shoes that pinch, and a "How are you?" when you don't really care.

These are a few of the masks, and we couldn't live without them. A tree couldn't live if we peeled all the bark away from it. With its insides thus exposed to the elements, the tree would perish. And people, too, would perish if they peeled away the bark of themselves and left inner souls naked to the elemental minds of their contemporaries.

So it is that I approve of the masks. How dull life would be if we couldn't participate in the game of seeing through the masks. How pleasant for our scientific minds if they could peel away the abstract behavioral masks of people, as they so easily peel away the bark of a defenseless tree and put its innards under a micro-scope for their sometimes brutal scrutiny.

Sigmund Freud peeled us with a curious, almost unmatched abandon, leaving our poets and novelists with a society too tender, too naked, too close to dying, to be touched.

And now we are growing new bark, I suppose, over the peeled places. We're looking for new masks, because we're not so defenseless as the trees, and we don't really care to understand each other, not nearly so much as we don't really want to be understood.

—**katey**

THERE is a quaint beauty as this quiet evening settles upon the day. I hear the birds rustling in the trees, and the faint calls of children as they spend their last energies before their baths and bedtime. The branches form gentle patterns in the subdued colors of twilight, and the cool breeze creeps into my open door.

Now is the hour of tranquillity. It is a special hour. It comes after a hectic day of quick thoughts, sudden decisions, and regimented seconds. As I puff on my pipe and the smoke stirs in lazy circles about me, it is a time for slow reflection and easy thoughts.

I wonder. What is the link between the earth and man? Do the moods of nature coincide with those of a human mind, meeting and blending in a coherent symphony?

I remember when I was a young boy and my twin brother and I slept under the stars. As we lay in the night, the bottomless dark was spotted with galaxies, and we were filled with a shaking awe. We gazed at those faraway suns and our souls shrank with the thought of boundless space, the far reaches of the universe that went on and on beyond our comprehension.

At that moment, both of us shared an unexplainable feeling: we were suspended in a gigantic mystery, bound on a tiny planet in a whirling, silent, infinite mass of beyonds and beyonds.

We wanted to talk to God, have Him open to our finite minds the beautiful and terrifying enigmas of life . . . and yet we were afraid of the knowledge He might impart. We were little boys taking on the universe, and the stars were in our hearts and eyes.

Tonight my son and his two friends are camping out in the woods. They are the same age that my brother and I were on that star-gazing evening.

What thoughts, as they hear the call of the whippoorwill, the scurrying of the night creatures, and the whisper of the wind, what thoughts are filling them? As they look into the night, do they feel the earth turn and the stirrings of the cosmos? Do they sense an affinity, a strange communion? Do they wonder, as we did years ago, about why they are here, who they are, and where they are going on this tiny grain of sand in a sea of stars?

I hope so. I hope this night gives them a glimpse of the universe's mysteries . . . and the mysteries within themselves.

Now it's time to shake the ashes from my pipe, turn to Katey, close the hour of tranquillity, and tell her of this mood, of this nearness to the twilight and its sounds and meaning.

And as we share our thoughts, there will come to us, I know, the feeling of another universe that is as mysterious and beautiful as the thousands of galaxies . . . the universe of ourselves. The wonder and the searching in this inner universe fills me with the same awe that I experienced long ago under a starry sky.

—ross

"WHEN I look at the night sky full of all those stars and realize how vast the universe really is, I feel like a little speck, don't you?"

"Nope."

The question came from a very young person, and the answer from a middle-aged one.

"You mean you're not awed by all that beauty out there?"

"No more than I'm awed by myself."

"You don't feel insignificant by comparison?"

"I'm no more insignificant than one of those stars out there. If anything, I'm likely to feel superior."

"Superior?"

The middle-aged person was neither cruel nor cynical. "There's one vast difference between me and one of those stars: I know the star's there, but the star doesn't know I'm here. I'm impressed at the sight of all those stars, but one of them, compared with all the others, is a mere speck, according to your feelings."

"You don't understand the wonder of it all," said the young one.

"It's certainly wondrous, but you're not going to talk me into feeling like an insignificant speck. There are only two reasons why you'd want to feel small when you look out there: either you're scared silly and need a hole to crawl into, or you prefer to think of yourself as insignificant so that you'll have a good excuse to avoid doing your homework."

"But you're missing the sheer beauty, the poetry of it."

"The poetry is in me, not in those stars. If I weren't here to react to them, they wouldn't exist."

"You're getting old."

"Yeah. Isn't that wondrous? I'll tell you what would really be wondrous."

"What?"

"Just one star out there. Just one in all that vastness. Just one star and one me. Really wondrous. Wondrously ridiculous."

—katey

Yesterday our daughter asked us an innocent question, and it opened a floodgate of memories. She didn't realize (and I didn't interrupt her absorbed thoughts) that this question shoved me back eighteen years.

This seventh-grade daughter, Kassy, was intrigued by a teacher who asked the class what democracy meant. He wasn't satisfied with the clichés, the many-mouthed phrases; he wanted to know from them what they really felt about "freedom."

Kassy asked Katey and me. I answered, "There are two things that freedom has given me: individual responsibility (the right of conscience) and dignity of man (self-respect)." Then the floodgate opened.

Dignity of man, the subtle phrase, took me back to Germany, where I was a prisoner of war eighteen years ago. It's very difficult to explain, this imprisonment in a place where a man's rights are dictated, his body is tortured, and his mind is usurped. It is difficult to say now, at this moment, that freedom became so precious it was an untouchable dream.

I was alone in a German military hospital with no American compatriots, and because my leg was amputated, I had no guard at my door. Many curious German soldiers visited me, and I had a unique chance to talk to them . . . after I had studied an American-German dictionary. I discovered the arrogant German; the SS torturer; the reluctant, educated soldier who resented Hitler; the simpleton; the wonderful simple man (the man who belongs to any country and who carries his soul like a banner); the blind patriot.

Freedom? I was the bird in the ungilded cage. The Germans? They were the birds in the gilded cage. The difference? Delusions had made most of the Germans believe that the cage was their rightful heritage: the censored word, the blinding loyalty to fatherland, the bowing to "might is right." The need for freedom choked me. I had known the dignity of man and the awful responsibility of self . . . of conscience about my actions and their effects upon others. I wanted, wanted, wanted it back—the chance to make up my own mind, to speak my own mind, to be responsible for my actions, to live and love for myself.

A few of the Germans felt the same way. They told me, behind cupped hands, with disguised gestures, and with painful eyes. They were prisoners too. They spoke to me in hushed tones, and they yearned—in a different way—for the freedom of speech, of action, and of mind.

We live so short a time upon this earth, so short, and the smile of a child, the kiss of your spouse, the lightning expression of your thought, the glint of sunshine on someone's hair, the quick push of grass, the warm handclasp of a friend, the genuflection to your God, the companionship of any book . . . all these are freedom's results, the outgrowth of man's search for goodness and greatness. These are the common things, the reaping of freedom's harvest. These are the things that I yearned for, when I was a prisoner of war, and they seared into me (the vision of them) until I built a fire of resistance that no torture or suffering could conquer.

If these words sound sentimental, they are. Freedom to me is a dual right, metaphysical and emotional. I learned, in those long months, that freedom is better practiced than espoused. It is better lived, consciously or unconsciously, than worded.

In February of 1945 I was repatriated, exchanged for German war prisoners. On a Swedish ship, the *Gripsholm*, I entered New York harbor. Bands were playing "Don't Fence Me In," and the New York skyline, with its wonderful architectural giants, appeared on the horizon. The Statue of Liberty suddenly came into view, like a mother opening a door for a hurt child. There were a thousand of us, homeless until now, and we cried. We cried without knowing exactly why, but actually knowing.

We were free. Not until we saw our lady of liberty, not until we saw the torch, did we really believe: the milkshakes, the loves, the green grass, the sudden thought, the quick kiss, the awful anguish of decision, the soft answer, the angry retort, the needful prayer . . . these were the freedoms we found again.

Someday I will be able to tell my Kassy about these freedoms. Someday I can go beyond "dignity of man" and say, "Freedom is a song, a love, a life—well respected and well nurtured."

—**ross**

Y ESTERDAY, when the feel of running was so full of goodness, did I feel the goodness, or did I catch it only now, today, remembering?

Is the aftertaste always the best taste? Must the good of now always wait for tomorrow, to come to fulfillment? And what does a person do about his last life's experience, when he can have no tomorrow to realize it?

I will tell you why people are urgent and careless about today's experience, why they keep one eye on the future, why they can't look too hard at today, why they would rather remember, look back, or look forward, than face the day at hand.

It's too much, that's why. We would keel over if we realized each other in any way but in the clouding of retrospect. For survival's sake, we put mists around each other.

If you were alone on the earth and suddenly came face to face with another human being for the first time, any human being, regardless of race, color, sex, age, or I.Q., you would stand there dumbfounded.

You would think it was remarkable. It would be almost too much for you to stand. If you had been alone, prior to this meeting, you would not know what you were, or who you were, and would probably not think about it. You would not know yourself, and therefore you would look upon another human being as astounding.

You would be overcome and inexpressive. Only after

the thing had gone would you come to realize, after many days, that you had been in the presence of something wonderful. And then you would begin to look at yourself and note comparisons, and in the looking, you would be afraid and even more alone than you were before.

We are too lonesome to love each other. People are as thick as dandelions on this earth. There are too many of us for any one of us to seem rare, until a season passes, and all the dandelions go to seed, as we knew they would, but kind of hoped they wouldn't, and hoped they would; and then comes the barren place of remembering, when we're cold and forlorn and have visions of a field of dandelions under a summer sun and know that we are nothing unless we can relate ourselves to someone else.

Every spring I come up blazing in a field of dandelions, and after the first blush of my personal blooming, I look around and find that I am surrounded by millions of like bloom and color, and after trying all summer long to distinguish myself, I go to seed in the fall.

The scattering of the seeds is the last effort at self-expression, but I know that each seed is different, that no matter where it blooms, it will not bloom me, but only its self. Even so, I will not look too carefully at the other dandelions, not even at those from my own seed, because to see them fully would extinguish me. They are too wondrous, and I am too vulnerable.

—katey

THE other day I wrote something about the dearth of insects around our property during the summer and early fall. I had forgotten about the crickets that kept me from falling asleep during warm nights.

Ross never hears the crickets unless I call his attention to them, and then he's annoyed because they keep him awake, too. I observed that when it was raining, and there were many rainy nights during the summer, the crickets were quiet. Or perhaps the rain sounds drowned them out.

What I said about the dearth of insects therefore still holds, because last summer I didn't lie in bed listening to them nearly so often as I have in past summers.

They kept me awake because they sounded as if they were indulging in their own special Morse code. I don't know whether the sounds were mating calls or just some stupid instinct. There was one right below our bedroom window that would "crick, crick, crick," and then from somewhere far down the alley would come an answering "crick, crick, crick."

Sometimes there would be four "cricks," and I'd listen carefully for the distant echo, and sure enough, four "cricks" came whispering down the alley in reply. The sounds put me in mind of Nelson Eddy and Jeannette MacDonald singing, "When I'm calling you-oo-oo-oo, oo-oo-oo," which is not exactly a lullaby tune.

Furthermore, I got the idea that they were the same two crickets every night I heard them, and I thought if this was a mating call, they were certainly taking their time about their courtship.

One night I muttered to the one in our back yard, "Oh, for pete's sake, hop over there to that other back yard and get it over with. You're nothing but talk, talk, talk, and that's no way to propagate your race."

From Ross's pillow came sleepy words, "Whadja say?"

"I'm not calling you-oo-oo," I replied. "Go back to sleep."

—katey

I saw a bleak film the other night in which grasshoppers and other insects chomped, methodically and unerringly, through vegetation until the plants were bare.

The commentator on this "Hellstrom Chronicle" projection was as bleak as the landscape. He told us that there are really only two survivors on this earth—the other animals are proportionately decreasing in number—and they are insects and man. I intentionally put the insects before man, because the commentator said we humans don't stand a chance.

You know, I felt like that poor man in front of the TV set, faced by the leering cigar-purveyor and being told smugly, "We're gonna getcha . . . maybe not now, but we're gonna getcha."

It was an eerie feeling, being told that the people who step behind us will be stepping less and less, until there is no clear call echoing between valleys . . . only the chomp-chomp-chomp of insects gnawing on what's left of this barren earth.

Why? I was informed that man has adapted somewhat to the changing environment, better than any other animal, but he doesn't adapt as quickly and fully as the insect. We may spray and kill the current insect population, but as suddenly as they die, there are a few who don't expire quite as quickly as we plan. From them, in a twinkling, there is passed to their offspring resistance to the pesticide we're using. And they start their eternal chomping again.

Another factor in their favor, I learned, was lack of emotion and thought. There is only the constant dedication to an instinctive duty: fight and survive.

All I could mutter was, "Life is more than this . . . far more than this, or life itself is the loneliest element of this universe."

After I mentally shook myself, like a dog trying to rid itself of fleas, I reflected on my life in this span of cosmos. It is as insignificant, I guess, as a lone insect piling up food for some mother-queen. We each breathe awhile.

But that isn't all, not by a long shot. I have a consciousness, way down to the utter depth of me and as far out as the world stretches. I can love with abandon or cry out to ghosts that haunt my nether moments. I can sense the beauty of a color or a thought. And my spirit, my ethos, can soar and wing toward delights.

I can really live. So, Mr. Insect, I'll agree to a delicate balance, but don't chomp over my soul. It's not palatable.

—**ross**

I AM alone now, at nearly midnight. There's a moon laced by the leaves of the big maple tree in our back yard, shimmering at me.

A six-year-old boy planted that tree there. He brought it home to his mother, a "flower" he had found in Hort Woods, and she planted it.

Now, more than thirty years later, its leaves pattern my vision of the moon, and I question the right of a long-ago six-year-old boy to block my way toward the moon.

Crickets are humming outside in the grass and shrubbery that are already turning subtly toward fall, mingling their dryness with the first few scattered leaves that remind me that I shall have to rake away the summer very soon again.

The girls, all my little girls, are sleeping now, with shiny clean hair rolled up in pins and curlers, ready for the first day of school tomorrow. My little boy took his own bath, all but his face and ears, and is off in sleep with his thumb and blanket.

There was a cow crying in the close-by university

But I missed, sometimes, the autumn in them, that period when all their color came forth for all it was worth. It's so quick a time, the autumn in us, because it's the last swift breath of spring and the lost hot breeze of summer.

I feel so tiny and so insignificant, not because of autumn, but because it came too close this year, because so many lovely leaves have fallen, and their falling has taken me unaware.

—**katey**

THE other night I heard the fall wind rustling . . . and it gave me a start, as it does each year.

I'm not prepared for the chill wind. I've had the warm sun on my back, the flowers blooming in our little flower bed, the nice feeling that summer will be with me forever. Then, suddenly, I hear the wind and feel the promise of cold, cold winter.

Oh, I know that summer will come again. I know that fall will astound my eyes with the golds, browns, yellows, and deep reds. I know that there is the vigor of crisp air sweeping leaves across my browning lawn. There is beauty in every season, and each one holds a fascinating moment.

But the symbol is there, isn't it? When I was young, I took each season for what it was: spring meant sprouting green and oiling of baseball gloves; summer brought free days—filled with wanton pursuits—and ice cream cones; fall introduced me again to the awful, wonderful hours of school and the hunt for horse chestnuts; winter was the time for snow forts, long, dark nights, study at the dining-room table, and taffy pulls.

Now I am middle-aged, and the first sound of the fall winds is disquieting. Today it is an omen. It speaks to me of middle age: that life moves relentlessly and that I'm closer to the final stages of winter and death.

Maybe that's why I, at this sudden chill, think of summer and warmth. I think of youth, its lack of thoughtfulness and breadth of spontaneity. There is no thought of tomorrow, no worry about a life span of frustrations. There is only the poignancy of today.

This mood of mine will change tomorrow with the loveliness of living. It will change with the eye-catching coloration and the spice of companionship.

But, now, the winds are rustling through me, and I want a word, a sign of comfort from the world about me. I want someone to say, "Here, you with a loneliness as stark as a bare maple, is a hand to warm you, a love to guide you, and a God to promise you."

I will get my wish tomorrow. There will be my family, my friends, even my dog, who will say these words in many ways and in many gestures.

I went out into the night to meet the wind. I looked at the stars, felt the wind pushing me, smelled the peculiar portent of fall leaves, and said to myself, "A soul may be as lonely as a star, but it burns as bright and as lovely."

As I came into the house, I wondered why I consoled myself with this observation . . . and then I knew. A life, as small as mine, may flicker and fade as a star, but within the sphere of its burning there is a conscious knowledge—and feeling—of its intensities and beauties.

Then I remembered what I said to myself when I was a springtime lad: "Any pain you may suffer, any disaster that may come, will be small when compared to the wonderful worlds that will open to you every day of your life."

And it's true, it's true.

Tomorrow, the fall wind will sing a different song.

—ross

I HAD some weird thoughts before going to sleep one night, and the next day I wrote them down so that I wouldn't forget them in case they might come in handy some day. I labeled them, "Thoughts to put down before someone else forgets them." Here they are:

Truth is essential to life. Life is all there is, and therefore it's important to know the truth about it, even if that knowing hurts or is impossible. The truth is there, and the problem is in finding it. It lies at the beginning of life, and all the history of life is contained within it.

It lies also in every mind because each of us began back there when the first primitive form of life moved upon the earth. There are those who say that life came from the sea, and there are some who believe that it began with a tiny plant like lichen. Perhaps it began from both, from a primitive amoeba in the sea and from a primitive lichen that clung to a rock of the earth and shimmered in the sun.

In the back of my mind there is a small, bright place where the red lichen lies dormant on a pebble of thought. I can see it there in my mind. In front of it is a shadowed labyrinth of recorded thoughts, mine and those of all mankind.

The truth is in the lichen, and I try to bring it out to you so that you can see it as my mind sees it, but it has so far to go in those shadows, in the darkened grooves, piled one upon another, circling, spiraling, moving up and down and left and right. What is left of the brightness comes to rest in my mind behind my eyes, and lies there, colorless and limp. I take it then, as tenderly as possible, and try to make it into words that you can hear and understand.

The words are not the lichen; they are representations of it, and when they reach your ears and rest behind your eyes, they become your words and mix with thoughts that you have chosen from your own recording.

Perhaps your mind's beginning lies in the sea where the amoeba was. We may have touched each other briefly without knowing.

And so I picture life's beginnings on a sunlit rock, where the red and shimmering lichen clings, and where the sea splashes up against the rock and a drop of the sea falls briefly upon the lichen. The drop evaporates and the lichen withers, but in that instant, too small for bringing to remembrance, two minds touched long ago and knew the truth of living.

—**katey**

T HE green of leaves lasts lushly all the long summer, but the yellow or red of them fades as quickly as a snowflake melting on a sleeve, as quickly as the warm comfort of childhood. There they are one day, brilliant and exciting in the October sunshine, and then suddenly they are gone, and the earth turns cold and gray.

Because they look their best in the glow of full sun, and because fog and rain too often cloud their beauty, and because the days, as one grows older, become shorter and less predictable, we skimmed out toward the mountains one evening just before the sun set.

The sun had dropped too far. It was too late in the day to see the bright, shimmering color in the full light and warmth of sunshine. The trees were lovely nevertheless. Twilight shadows were creeping over the valleys, edging their way toward the mountaintops, and in the half light, half shadow, the color seemed subdued and gentle.

I wonder how it would seem to me if I found myself on the earth for the first time, as the adult that I am, but without memory of any other autumn, or any other day or night. How would I react to the sinking sun, the brilliant colors, the creeping shadows of twilight? And when the shadows drifted slowly into the only dark night of my experience, how would I feel?

Would I curl up like rabbits and squirrels, closing the night beneath tired lids, or would I be terrified that the light had gone and might never come back again? Would I shrink toward the ground in terror, clutching the trunk of a tree, and quiver all the night through, or would I sleep?

How would it be to come across the first night? How would it be without experience and memory?

However it would be, the coming dawn, the first faint glimmer of light coming back again, even if the day was foggy or full of rain, would be worth the terror or the solid sleep of the first knowledge of night.

How splendid the earth would seem at high noon! How particularly splendid if one viewed his first day on earth in a warm October sun, surrounded by brilliantly colored trees! And how melancholy the second coming of night would seem, how pointless, and how monotonous.

I don't relish the thought of being accustomed to autumn, and it bothers me to become too accustomed to being alive. After all, the leaves, despite their current brilliance, are really falling.

—**katey**

THE other night my daughter came home from her residence hall at the university, shivered with the cold in her bones, and said, "Daddy, build me a fire."

We had just thrown a cord of wood in the cellar for the long winter evenings, so I commandeered the houseful of kids to make the trek from cellar to hearth with arms full of logs.

"Let me see, now," I muttered to myself as I began my yearly ritual, "a good backlog, some kindling and paper, another good log in front, a smaller one for the fiery pyramid . . . and, whoosh, let's see if she 'ketches.' "

I leaned humbly toward the fireplace, lit the first kindling of the season, and there it was: one of the loveliest, warmest sights in the world. Perhaps the cool of fall, edging aside the hot of summer, invites the mind and spirit toward a hearth. A leaf falls, the wind stirs, a chill settles in the marrow, and as one warmth leaves I yearn for another.

Then my daughter sings into the room, "Daddy, light me a fire," which also meant "Light my heart." And I did.

As I watched the flames climb and smelled the acrid wood smoke, I wondered why one season ebbs and another eases into being, as one mind and soul has its seasons . . . and each season of existence ebbs and eases in the same way. There is one difference, I reflected. And I must ask my older friends about this: I know that my physical being has one cycle: spring, summer, fall, and winter; but my ethos has an eternal cycle . . . and I move from season to season with the same abandon that turns the earth.

As long as I live, my heart will sing with spring, leap with summer, tumble with the leaves in fall, and glow by the fireside of winter. As long as I live, why can't my mind churn with wonderful, mysterious cyclings of man and earth spinning with dreams and stars?

So, in the autumn of living, when my daughter calls to me to light her a fire, why can't I light her the world?

—ross

WHERE'S the most beautiful place in the world?

There are four that are equally beautiful. Two are at the corners of people's mouths, and the other two are at the corners of their eyes, where laugh wrinkles are etched on a face.

The older a person grows, the deeper the grooves run at the four corners of his living, and the more contentedly the laughs can flow.

How many lovely old faces I've seen, faces with grooves deep enough to hold years of laughter, faces sprinkled all over themselves with tiny wrinkles, each wrinkle coming and going, holding and letting go, letting laughter come in and go out again, like a day that's part rain and part sun, like an intricately shadowed woods speckled softly with sunlight.

Laughter has come to these faces and taken its place there and held on, deeply, groovingly, movingly, lovingly.

I know too well that living flesh doesn't keep, but how lovely it becomes the older it grows, and how much the ancient grooves give back to us the love and laughter of being, and how well the four lovely corners teach the young, the little ones, how to handle their rosy faces and where to put the grooves.

Love makes the laughter, and laughter makes the lovely, holding grooves, the deep, the subtle gutters, where a chuckle can run its course and end at the corner of an eye as a sunlit drop of a smile.

The most beautiful place in the world is a human mind that, out of its own intricate etchings of thought and experience, can put smile wrinkles at the four vital corners of its face, two at the edges of the mouth, and two at the corners of the eyes.

—katey

5 A season of reckoning

HERE I am with an absolutely delicious zucchini/
macaroni/spaghetti-sauce casserole, leftover, and no
one has died. No one died from eating it, but that isn't
what I have in mind.

It's perfectly good, and if there were a sudden funeral in the neighborhood, I'd have it ready to take to
the bereaved. I was brought up in what is probably now
known as the "old tradition" of taking food to the
household where someone has died and the persons left
are too grieved and too busy to cook.

It's probably a good custom that is still going on,
but our neighborhood gets younger and younger, and
there are fewer and fewer occasions under these old
trees when I can sally forth with my life-preserving
casseroles.

Many years ago, in the autumn, two persons died,
and the families of both needed casseroles. I made two
large meat loaves and two huge from-scratch casseroles
of escalloped potatoes. It takes time to put those ingredients together, especially the potatoes, and then let
them sit in the oven for two hours.

While they were cooking away those two hours, I

went outside and began to rake leaves like a madwoman. I, too, was bereaved. With every flick of my rake, gathering all the yellow, red, and brown leaves together, I was mentally raking together the lovely, colored lives of the persons I mourned, and when I was vicious with that rake, I was mentally cursing disease and pestilence and all the half-tinted obnoxious people who had helped my persons die.

And Ross came outside to the lawn, and he said to me, "These people are counting on your dinner. When will those dinners be ready?" And so I quit the raking and viciousness and storming about dying, came inside, took my casseroles from the oven, wrapped them carefully, and made sure, with hot pads, that Ross wouldn't burn himself while he transported my tradition-loaded casseroles to the bereaved.

And I, too, felt better because I had done something. It wasn't much to do in the face of death, but I had done it. Not until now has it helped me very much to release those persons who died and feel any sort of comfort from what I did.

And here I am now, confronted with a lovely zucchini/macaroni/spaghetti-sauce casserole, fit for a funeral. And nobody wants to die for it.

—**katey**

I LOOKED out my window today and saw the leaves cascading from the beautiful cathedral of trees on our street, and a moment of truth hit me.

Autumn, I told myself, is the season of reckoning. Winter withers the soul, spring swamps the senses, and summer seethes with the passion for living, but autumn carries a swift message. It says, as leaf after leaf falls, "Your days are numbered as the leaves, and they fall and there is no return."

The first impact of this thought, I confess, shook me, as a slight, imperceptibly chilling wind scurries the leaves and warns of the relentless gusts of winter. Life, I mused, is so short, and why isn't there time enough, world enough, to hold me here?

Why must I, when I feel the keen blessings of living, when with age I know the kiss of life fully, when my mind has been mellowed with experience and excited with a thousand stimuli, must I depart from this beautiful consciousness and fall, like a leaf, and be forgotten in a million other autumns? I'd like to share all of them.

Is there an injustice and a curious kismet that befalls man? Why does he love, feel the ecstatic ranges of emotion, watch the brilliance of a sunrise, catch the warm thought of a friend, smell the fragrance of a rose, soak in the warmth of a fire on the hearth, sense the beauty of a glance, lose himself in the words and books of gracious men, fill himself to the brim with the wonders . . . and then fall like a leaf, an unknowing pattern of protoplasm?

A mind can churn with these unanswerable, awful questions. They lead to a finality that is unbearable, to an insensitivity when all of one's being is filled with sensitivity, so tender and so moving.

I am a small man and can be moved by winds, winds as slight as a gentle breath, and I know that such wind will shake me from my tree one of these short days. It may come during this season of reckoning.

However, I said to myself after I was shaken by that moment of truth, the puzzle continues, but so does life and loveliness. Where I fall, another leaf grows. It would be small comfort to me if I did not care for beauty and yearn for all those who share it with me and will share it in the eons to come.

While I live and cling to my tree of life, there is all of me seeking fulfillment, striving for a thought or a word or a love that is more than yesterday, less than tomorrow. So, with this mystery of life plaguing me, I must savor in my autumn as much of this vast panorama of existence as I can hold within me.

I will harvest my loves with care.

—ross

M Y sister once said, when she was trying hard to remember something, "It's on the tip of my verge, and I can't think of it." She had her phrases confused, but everyone knows how she felt. She had trouble getting to sleep because of that one little thing she couldn't remember.

Now I'm having an even greater difficulty. This time it's not only a poem but the author as well. I believe it was a French author and that the poem is called "Art." I remember well the man who gave me a specially typed copy of it when I was twenty-two and how I kept it in my unorthodox files for many years.

I even remember some of the lines: "Stronger and more sound than brass remains the sovereign song," and "Chisel, carve, and file, until thy vague dream imprint its smile upon the unyielding flint."

I needed that poem desperately the other day when my daughter was bemoaning the fact that beautiful people with beautiful thoughts create great works of art, and the people themselves disappear forever and nothing but what they said or left behind them remains.

She resented the idea that such minds should have to become dust, so to speak. I sympathized, because I had been reading a biography of Kate Hepburn and had examined a photograph of her lovely, chiseled face, and I hated the thought that those lovely bones would disintegrate and leave the world forever.

I wanted the poem to explain to my daughter,

however falteringly, that we love also the beauty of certain butterflies and birds, and sometimes we preserve them by one manner or another. And people, too, often leave the best of what they had behind them, despite Shakespeare's words, "The good is oft interred with their bones."

Whole civilizations have died, and when archaeologists dig, they find evidence of real people, good and bad, and I suppose that gives them a better perspective on their own short lives, although I doubt that anyone overcomes the personal resentment at turning back into dust.

That's why I like the line about the "vague dream," of all things, implanting a mere "smile," of all fleeting things, upon such a thing as unyielding as a piece of rock or flint. But many drops of water round stones into smooth pebbles, and many dreams can create wonders upon rock.

—katey

THERE is a great similarity between birth and death in the intensity of emotion. There is turbulence at the beginning of either experience, and after a time there is a deep peace, a quiet poignancy, a knowledge that needs no expression.

A long time ago I wrote a poem about motherhood, and later another one about death, the first close death of my life. In a later, more rational mood, I concluded that neither of the things I had written was a poem at all, but that they might stand as prose, as small prose, that would be to the world of words as a single breath is to all the windstorms of the earth.

Taken out of its poetic form, this is how the "first death" poem goes:

"In the beginning, in the egocentric pain, death was

a circle, black and moving; I was in the center and the rim kept closing in, folding darkness over strangers first, then friends, then those related distantly, then you, of my flesh, and I was selfish. I couldn't let you go alone. I was afraid.

"Your heart and mine had beaten first in the same womb, although at different intervals, and I claimed the stopping of your heart as mine: the rim was closing in.

"Then I came out of my heart and into the world. I stood beside a pond, a little pond, where one large stone cast into its water made a gigantic splash and many ripples.

"Holding the stones, soothed by the gentleness of time, I watched the ripples, and the movement of the rim of dying changed. You were the stone I tossed into the pond, and there was beauty in the quiet ripple of the waters, where the sun cast light and shadows.

"Your stone made dancing, colored lights, moving ever outward in a gay and lively pattern. Before it reached the bank, I tossed another stone, and then another, and the ripples moved, pursued, and merged with yours, until the pattern was not yours, nor mine, nor anyone's.

"I tossed a handful then of little pebbles, and I do not know (the dancing sparkles were so mixed and merged) just when yours reached the bank. But I knew that somewhere in the ripple of your life, I was there, with countless other pebbles, unrelated, and that if no one lives alone, then no one dies alone, and that no pond is ever still, unless the earth itself is still."

—katey

ONE day last summer, Katey and I stood on the

veranda of our Maine vacation hotel watching a wild twilight.

As the red sun glanced off the rocky coast, a bagpipe player mixed his wailing, strident melody with the plaintive cries of sea gulls nesting on nearby Gull Island. It was an eerie and unusual moment.

I thought then, as the brilliant seascape blended with the strange chorus, of other moments that mingled in my life, quick episodes that make up my tapestry of living. It reminded me of Virginia Woolf's comment, "All human beings are concerned with this: that the whole world is a work of art; that we are parts of the work of art.

There was the first time I held my newborn daughter in my arms. I was filled with a tenderness—this tiny, fragile baby against my shoulder—that embraced the sudden thoughts of love and protection.

It was a contrast to a few years before, when death was snuffing out life faster than I could envision. I was on my first bombing mission, over Ploesti, and flak and fighter planes were knocking our Flying Fortresses into blazing hells. Fear was all-encompassing.

I thought again of when I was young, when my twin brother and I decided to sleep on our lawn under a starlit sky. As we gazed at Orion, the vastness of the universe filled us with wonder . . . what is beyond and beyond, where and how did the world begin, and how did miniscule, insignificant individuals like us evolve? And picking up a stray leaf, we marveled at the "inner" universe and its intricate cellular structure in contrast to the unfathomable outer universe.

That moment reminded me of another one that occurred a year before, when I suddenly discovered that "I" was I. It was an excruciating minute. The discovery of my own conscience, my cocoon of life and thought so distinct from any other, was too much for me to bear. I walked for an hour or more around the dining-room table in bewilderment, fear, and delightful awareness. Never again have I so felt that life was tingling my very fingertips.

Then there was that hour when Katey and I sat in our living room and there was a unique silence between us. We were very aware of each other, but a peculiar ease, a distinct feeling of comfort and being together—each with his own thoughts—permeated us. We were one . . . and two. And then there was that second when both of us spoke, and we knew, down to the core of a single thought, the soul and breadth of that thought. It was a rare and beautiful understanding.

There are many instances that wove that tapestry: the leaping of a trout in a lonely, whispering stream, the blending of our family's voices at Christmas, the chilling mystery of a poignant death, the first time I saw Katey after my return from a prison camp and the ludicrous hopping on one leg to embrace her, the uncontrollable laughter that convulsed our family over a now-forgotten incident . . . and on and on.

These have framed my work of art, and they have splashed plentifully into the colors of my life.

—ross

Ross and I have been thoroughly shaken by a close friend's death. We loved him long and dearly, for deeply personal reasons, as we love his wife and children and the rest of his family.

We have, of course, been similarly shaken. Nobody can reach the age we've attained without being shaken. I don't know about Ross, but I'm often a little surprised, after being shaken until I thought the whole universe had suddenly become lopsided, when I find that not long afterwards I am living through a routine, too relaxed, and insufferably dull day.

What shook us most about losing this friend was the fact that anyone with such life in him could end. It's incredible that such an effective and penetrating personality, such lively humor, and such great warmth and kindness could suddenly disappear . . . poof . . . gone . . . all over . . . ended.

Death is a dark and introverted condition, but the darkness and introversion are not often a truly accurate portrayal of the life that has gone. Fresh grief is sore and self-centered, raw and agonizing. The softness of it comes only when the grief-stricken come back to thinking of the whole life, lived individually, that is now gone, and not only the part of that life to which they clung.

A man's soul and life are his own, and even if he gives himself away in hundreds of careful and loving pieces, he's still his own man with his own life span, and no one but he has a claim on it, except his own God.

It is for the beloved pieces of people that we grieve, and for our own raw wounds when those pieces are severed. The deeper the love and attachment of those pieces, the greater the wound and the longer the healing.

When a man has accepted the unexpected difficulty of living out a life, however brief or unfulfilled, we cannot do him the discourtesy of dwelling only upon his death. We must recover from our grief as quickly as possible, so that we can think about him as he was in his whole life, for the sake of the dignity of his life, and for the preservation of what he gave to us before he died. It is our grief, after all, not his, and his life is worth more than our sighs or tears.

—katey

W HAT in the world do you say to a blue-eyed eleven-year-old who has suddenly discovered that she's alive, and because of being alive, that she will one day die?

What do you say when she comes to you, scared by the universe?

I remember writing a phrase, when I was twelve, "I held a cat in my arms and discovered life." I tried to explain that phrase to my own child, that holding a pet means life to a human hand. I wanted her to think about life, living, not death.

Her father, who came close to death at one time, values life so much that he speaks of it daily, his love of life. I do, too, not because I've been near death, but because I've lived here on this earth with all its goodness, because I was born to see and hear, and to smell and taste, and to feel the wondrous softness of newborn babies.

She was fifteen minutes old when they gave her to me, as I lay on the hospital litter. I was awake, and she hadn't been cleaned up. They had wrapped her in a receiving blanket and handed her to me. I held her, and she cried. I patted her tiny arm and held her close, and when I nestled her, she stopped crying.

She has braces on her teeth now, and I haven't nestled her much. I've made her clean and comfortable, but I haven't nestled her much lately because she is much of a child and needs her own life.

Now, suddenly, after eleven years, she has discovered life and I have to cuddle her again.

And that's why I said to her, "When I held you inside of me, I worried about birth and whether I would live to see you, but I kept thinking of all the billions of people born to the earth, and all the billions of mothers who felt pain when their little people were born, and I thought that if they could do it, I could, too."

Then Ross showed her an October moonlight slanting through the autumn leaves, and one lone star through the branches of an elm.

And then I said to her, "If your great-grandfather can die, or if one of my dearest friends can die, or if your friend's father can die, then I can, and you can, too, just like all the beloved people out of history. I am not yet ready to die, but I will be ready some day, and I will do it, just as surely as I gave birth to you, and you must remember that you can do anything I can do."

Then I sent her off to bed, saying to one who had just discovered life, "Hit the sack, baby."

—katey

THE contrast between a freshman and a professor emeritus provides people of State College with a long view of life that is often denied to those who live elsewhere. We are close to the seasons, too, in Centre County, and their contrasts blend with our way of living.

This fall I was one of three generations, like three seasons, who went into the mountains for a final checkup on my father's cabin before the winter. Our three-year-old, Amy, fell asleep in the car on the way over and remained sleeping while my professor-father cleared the grounds around the cabin.

The leaves were still falling then, and there was an ominous tang in the wind that blew through them. Amy, of the generation of spring, was blissfully unaware of life. I, of the generation of summer and approaching fall, made a note of the quick passing of time, and my father, of the generation of late fall and approaching winter, was decisive and brisk in his activities. He worked rings around me, not wasting energy on the sadness of the end of things.

I was thinking, "I have always wanted adventure,

but everyone else has gone far and wide, and I have always been close to home. I keep myself safe here in the green mountains, where loneliness is not an unusual thing, where the whippoorwill sings to himself at dusk, where leaves fall silently and alone, where twigs drop gently to the ground and life knows birth and death in the seasons and goes on without asking to be seen or heard.

"I would have been better as a tree or a violet or even as a rounded stone at the bottom of a brook, nameless, unseeking, unremembered. We are all these things. We are the stones and stars and whippoorwills, and we are no more, no less, than all these, because everything is the same thing. Melt me down, and I am earth, or air, an atom caught in the whirl of the universe, nothing and everything, as the universe is everything and nothing."

While I was sitting there thinking, I heard a quiet cricking, and I looked carefully, in great detail, through the stones, moss, and fallen leaves. I found it then. It was a katydid. Its wings, moving stiffly, made two small membranes at the tips move against each other to make a sound. I called my father.

"Yes," he said, casually, "it's cold. When the air is chilly, they get cold, and they can hardly move. It's old, too. It's dying of cold and old age."

He picked it up carefully and put it on a branch of a hemlock tree nearby. The katydid could hardly grasp the needles to take hold. It stopped cricking, putting all its strength into holding on.

"It looks like a leaf," I said, thinking of the greenness and fine white lines of its wings.

"Yes," he said, smiling. "It's turning brown."

Then I noticed the brown spots on the wings, probably the result of experience rather than age. I remembered that katydids I had seen in the early spring were a brilliant, almost cocky green and there were no brown spots to mar their brilliance. My impulse was to tramp on this one, to end the process, to prevent any further chilling and discomfort for this thing that was once so green and so lively.

But my father's hands had been gentle and decisive when they picked up the katydid without hesitation and placed it on the tree, where no one could tramp on it. My father's hair was white; mine was merely streaked; and I thought of the unawareness of the downy-haired child in the car.

Because the green in me was still showing, I might have taken that katydid's destiny into my hands by putting my foot on it, in the guise of mercy. I might not have had the wisdom to let it finish its life in its own way.

The wind was stronger now, dusk was coming, and my father had finished his chores. I turned as we left, for a last look at the katydid, who still clung to the hemlock branch, which swayed now in the wind.

"Hang on, Professor Emeritus," I said to it softly. "Stay with us. There's a new crop of freshmen coming in soon, and there's more green, latent and promised, under this leaf-browned, wind-swept earth."

And as I left, it was still holding on.

—katey

Here in this place 6

THE day of Thanksgiving is one that traditionally engenders gratitude for our unique heritage and sums up—in one day of the year—our blessings in being free and saucy, individually and collectively, as Americans. However, I feel more like a free-blown individual today, and my thanks are bottled up in this essence of being, of living within and without myself.

So, I am grateful . . .

. . . for breath, the simple delight of taking a deep, fulfilling breath.

. . . for holding within my mind a thought that touches a single person with tenderness and love.

. . . for reaching out, on a sparkling spring day, and holding a daffodil against the green grass and a blue sky.

. . . for feeling the earth move under me—in a strange, mysterious moment—and sensing the universe expanding and contracting, like a man breathing his way through a day or an eternity.

. . . for the sound of a whippoorwill in a hushed glen and the rustle of a gentle wind in a quiet forest.

. . . for the leap of a trout at twilight, the gleam of

pink on his belly and the pale sunset reflected in the ripples of the mountain stream.

. . . for the awesome stillness of an empty cathedral, and the eerie feeling that thousands upon thousands of silent prayers are crowding to the rafters and beyond.

. . . for the strident tones of a Beethoven symphony and the sweet, simple folk tune that envelops the heart.

. . . for the warmth that emanates from the hearth in our home and the golden flames sparking from the logs and into my mind.

. . . for the quick smile of a friend, the uninhibited giggle of a child, and the hearty guffaw of a teenager.

. . . for the fleeting minutes that I live and the beauties that these minutes lay before my feet.

—ross

ONCE a long time ago, on a path lit by the yellow-gray shadows of a fog, where a street light looked like a circling of spider webs, a very young man told me that he wasn't afraid of getting old.

I said I was. I told him that I was terrified of getting old. I said that getting older and ever older meant something sallow and yellow, shadowed by the black of dying that comes so closely after getting old. I was thinking about tomorrow then, when I was so tenderly young, and he was thinking about being young, and before.

I suppose he hadn't examined spider webs very closely, as I did when I was young, and he couldn't see how pale and thin the single webs were, and thereafter it would never occur to him to think that the light around a lamp in the fog could have any relationship to a spider web, or to getting old.

The awful thing about him was that he came to look like Cary Grant, the older he got, and he came to have five or six kids to my four, except that I bore them and he didn't, but that's not quite fair. A man bears his children the way a woman does in a different way. A man takes all the hurt and sense of being, just the way a woman does, but he does it differently.

What grabs at my throat is that he didn't know, when he was young and hadn't yet become a Cary Grant, that the still fog-light around a street lamp is the spider web of being, of being a still soul surrounded by, encircled by, the threads of other lives. He wasn't then the least bit interested in his own getting old.

I suspect that he takes an interest now, especially in the green, tender shoots of his own being, the seeds he put out to perpetuate himself, and in the thin shreds, the delicate, circular threads that surround him and the people who came before him. I suspect that he's right in the middle of a spider web or a lamplight in the fog. I'd guess that he's wiggling in the web of middle age.

"I do not like," I told him in the fog and in the tenderness of youth, "to think of the flesh of my face, that lingers on the front of my mind, going bad or getting withered."

I am forever so. I would like to think that the young man could be forever Cary Grant, in his face or what his eyes tell me. I would like to keep him from getting old and then dying away from me.

My throat hurts worst when I think that he's coming around to the edge of the lamplit circle, in the same fog or spider web of being, and finding himself somewhere on the edge of a circle, and fading out into the universe.

—katey

REMEMBER the wind Wednesday night? It "whoeeed"

through the leafless trees and seemed to roar, "Wait! You haven't heard anything yet."

This wind reminded me of a night when I was aboard a Liberty Ship bound for Italy. A gale was howling and no one was allowed on deck because the ship was rolling, if I recall correctly, about forty degrees.

Another chap and I disregarded the regulations and sneaked up on deck. The wind roared through the top structure with that same peculiar "whoeee," and it thrilled and terrified us at the same time. We were lost and overwhelmed by the sound, but the terrible might of the wind fascinated us with its portent of awful danger.

It said the same thing to us: "Wait! You haven't heard anything yet."

What is it about the wind? One time it wails like a siren of foreboding, but the next it wheels playfully among the trees.

Tuesday evening I felt the strong pulls of nature, of colorful autumn thumbing its nose at somber winter, and within the holds of our house, Katey and I laughed at the bellows of the wind and the protesting creaks of the trees.

The Wednesday wind was different: it meant business. "Get ready, you flimsy, weak mortal, you," it roared, "because the cold, cold drafts of me are going to numb your spirit and blast your house."

That was enough for me. The next morning I put in a call for fireplace wood, inspected the northwest windows, and took the car to the garage for a change to snow tires.

Mentally, I readied myself. I thought over the books I'd like to read by my hearth, conjectured about the games my restless children would like to play on a wintry night, and even inspected the hall closet to see if my muffler was there.

Our dog was uneasy, too, with that natural instinct about change. The wind made strange noises for him, and his ears curled back as he moved uncertainly from one chair to another.

Okay, Mr. Wind, I've got the message. But may I ask one small favor of you?

Will you, kindly and always, be at my back?

—ross

T HIS column is recommended for adults only. Anyone who can't read is advised to refrain from trying to do so in this particular column, because I'm too sentimental to disillusion anyone.

Who was the dirty bird who first told you that there was no Santa Claus? Or were you like me, suspicious about it but not quite wanting to disbelieve, until the evidence was so great that you had to admit it to yourself?

My disbelief came from some very sophisticated friends I had in third grade. They were so disillusioned that they wanted to yell at all the believers, in a childish singsong, "You believe in Santa Claus! Ya-ya-ya-Oh-ya-ya!"

I can remember when my older sister, eighteen months older than I, had an argument with my parents about it. She said that it was "absolutely impossible" for a man with a sleigh and reindeer to cover the entire earth in one evening and go down all those chimneys with all those toys for children all over the earth and get it all finished in one night, and that there wasn't a bag big enough to hold it all, let alone reindeer to haul it around, and so on.

My parents didn't know that I was listening, but I

remember that they tried to convince her, even though they knew it was too late. Fairy tales were "out," as far as my sister was concerned. She's the one who went upstairs one afternoon, when the fairy had forgotten to put a nickel under my pillow for a tooth, and came down saying softly and sweetly, "The fairy was just leaving as I went into your bedroom."

I looked skeptical but I wanted to believe. I was one of those quiet, introspective children who love to imagine that they see elves or pixies. I can remember looking into a small pool in a stream in Bear Meadows and seeing tiny nymphs diving into that pool and swimming about, then climbing up on the little rocks to dry themselves in the pools of sunlight falling from the hemlock trees.

They slept in acorn shells on bits of soft, green moss, which they had gathered during the day, and they spent days eating teaberries to sustain themselves. I had quite an imagination in my little-girl days, and I don't like people who tell the little ones that there's no Santa Claus.

Maybe Santa isn't everywhere, but wherever good parents are, he's there, and I rather enjoy the fact that I've never heard any adult tell any little one that there is no such thing. It's a secret kept, like the Easter Bunny, for every small child by all kind people who live with that special tradition.

How old must you be before the illusions crumble? Oh, let's say maybe in second or third grade, where some people are more sophisticated and less imaginative and perhaps a little sad.

Did I ever tell you that whenever you walk past a cricket and it stops cricking, you've missed seeing a pixie? I've missed so many pixies that way. I suppose I don't walk softly enough, or believe hard enough.

—**katey**

Amy made a Christmas card for her father, and it was all tinsel and stars and full of pictures. And in her own printing were the topsy-turvy words "Bells will be ringing, and you will be singing."

She was right. Bells rang, and her daddy sang. Looking at her eight-year-old efforts, I wondered why I hadn't drawn any of my artless pictures since I was thirteen or so. Just for the heck of it, I began to draw.

I drew a car, front view, and asked Ross if he knew what it was. He did, and that gave me courage. I drew a lady, a horse, a turkey, and an overweight woman, but when one of my children drew a horse, I decided that her horse was better than mine and that I'd better give up trying to draw. (Ross gave it up years ago, and he drew a very cockeyed horse, just to show us why.)

I thought to myself, okay, if my kid can write that bells are ringing and you'll be singing, I can write verse, too. I started a game of verse writing. I wrote, "Snow is to shovel, leaves are to rake, grass is for mowing, and love is a fake."

"Write me a poem, Ross," I said. Dutifully, because Ross can't resist games or competition of any kind, he sat with a pencil and a couple of pieces of paper, and he kept trying long after the children had gone to bed and the fire on the hearth was burning out.

Finally he said, "I'm sorry, but I can't write this," and he handed me what he had written. He had written, "Where do I live? I live in this place, this place— where—where my—" and then trailed off. I looked over at him, at the kindly grin-wrinkles at the corners of his mouth, at the quiet, comforting hazel eyes, and I thought I could see his heart beating for the sake of life, for the love of it, and I thought I'd better help him to finish his poem.

That's why, looking at him, and keeping him con-

stantly in mind, I wrote this, which he began and had
inside of him and gave to me:

> Where do I live?
> I live here in this place, where my small son smiles
> suddenly,
> and the hearth-light leaps
> to his grin.
> I live here, where my heart
> beats out in poignance
> toward the eyes of my wife.
> I live in this place,
> where an elfin blue-eyed girl dances,
> flickering in and out of my mind,
> as my breath goes—in and out—
> and then catches itself and holds on for an instant.
> I live in the scattered, bright words
> of my pretty girls.
> I live here in this place,
> where dust is too lively
> to settle down to earth.
> I live where the young things grow,
> the green things, like my love,
> my love of where I live,
> here, now, and in this place.

And then I said, "Ross, this is not good. It doesn't
rhyme. But I tried to catch your thinking, and I have no
right to your thinking, and so it's yours, all yours, and
never mine."

And that's a fact. Nothing I ever truly loved, like
my husband, children, changes in the seasons, music,
bird songs, age creeping onto a woman's hands, silence
and then the quiet plat of snowflakes or the slip of
raindrops, or the quick glance of an old friend, has ever
really belonged to me. Nothing I see is mine forever,

because I am no more forever than a snowflake or a shooting star.

Yet sometimes I try to catch the shooting stars, and that's why I tried to finish Ross's poem.

—katey

Each new year I've made a list of resolutions and broken most of them before January was over. But it was fun . . . trying to live up to those I didn't break and mildly regretting those I slipped past.

However, this New Year's Eve I feel slightly glad to let the old year slide by, and I'm a little tired of maintaining the few resolutions that are left. There have been a few trials, a few tribulations, a few mishaps during the past year that make me want to sit and weave some wishes instead of climbing up a stair of resolutions.

So, here goes a tapestry of dreams:

I wish for laughter, flowing free as the riffles in a brook and high as a trout leaping for a fly at twilight.

I wish for hope, as far as the nearest star and as wide as the Milky Way.

I wish for faith, as simple as a dog's listening for the call of his master and as deep as a child's calling in her sleep for her mother.

I wish for happiness, not so full that the heart would burst but not so seldom that one waits anxiously for a precious moment to arrive.

I wish for charity, especially from God, then from my friends, because I know not what I do sometimes; and sometimes when I know what I do, that's the time I need their charity most.

I wish for words, words to tell what's in the heart of me when I'm speechless, when the world is too big and the voice too small.

I wish for patience, for bearing my little and gigantic eccentricities through their day-by-day expressions and their swinging climaxes that carry frustrations on an uncertain pendulum.

I wish for concern, for people to care, not only for me but for the whole aspect of living, from the barefoot, starving child of India to the daring pioneer of our space age.

I wish for tolerance, a great wide tolerance that embraces all of mankind, that imbues the black with good regard for the white and fills the white with the same wide view, and for a world divided to become a world united.

I wish for understanding, from a tiny thought that blossoms into an all-encompassing fulfillment, to a great truth that breaks into tiny petals and touches everyone.

I wish for beauty, the gleam of a fire on the hearth, the first green of spring, the smile of a child, the rare colors of a rainbow, the glance of my wife's eyes, the orange-blue of a sunset, the awesome cascade of a waterfall, the stirring strains of a Brahms symphony, the minute-by-minute essence of living.

I wish for love, the wonderful grace of love, which flows, moves, surrounds, envelops, and is the single best reason to dream of laughter, hope, faith, happiness, charity, words, patience, concern, tolerance, understanding, and beauty. And in love we find the answer to all our wishes.

—ross

The covering over 7

Northern-bound people, without too much reason, think of themselves in terms of the season. Whenever it's cold, they think that they're old, and when it gets hot, they think that they're not. In spring they take wing, and in fall they all bawl.

Much of their gladness, too much of their sadness, is bound without reasons to changes in seasons. Changes in weather bring them together, winter arthritis or springtime bursitus, summers of asthma and autumns of plasma.

Rhyme takes time, and I have very little of either. Therefore I shall come straight to the point, of which there is also very little, and say what I have to say without fiddle-de-daddling around.

If winter is a symbol of age or of death, which day of winter would I choose to mark the end of my living? Winter, as the end and the covering over of green growing things, is composed of many separate pieces of days and moments.

Shall I choose a day in which gently falling snow-flakes cover a dirt road in the woods while the sun shines slantingly and hauntingly through the trees and the brush? Shall I choose a blizzard, the kind that beats upon my face and pushes at my back and swirls and whistles and makes the trees look small and shakes forgotten nests from their branches?

Shall I go away on a great big snowflake day when all the flakes are stars and gathered together in stardust heaps on anything stationary, on things that never get looked at otherwise, like telephone wires, empty branches, benches, pipes, outdoor water fountains, garbage-pail lids, roofs, rain spouting, the tops of evergreen trees, and the back fenders of cars?

Shall I fall by the wayside on one of those slushy days when the streets are wet and guttered with blobs of soot-laden, tired snow, and the pointed ends of icicles are dripping from spouting, and the constant, rhythmic dripping sounds and smells like spring?

Shall I choose a frozen-quiet, crust-snow day when the sun is out, and the snow that has already fallen has become brittle and still, and so have the roads and walks and trees, all frozen stiff right where they were, until I walk on them and the day, and they crackle, and the breath that comes out of me freezes?

I have many faces. So does winter. So does every day. If I am old this winter, which winter day, of all the long winter days, suits me best?

—**katey**

I DON'T like winter.

The cold strikes my bones, and the stark trees haunt me. I want the warm days and the smells of spring and summer.

Yet, on Sunday, I grudgingly nodded to winter. It was a day that one must acknowledge, whether he likes it or not.

The wind howled, the snow beat against the windows, the cold invaded the house, and I felt it creep into every crevice. Winter had its day, and what a day it was!

I built a fire. I joked to my family. I sang about warm days and warm loves. I turned the furnace thermostat up a notch . . . but I kept one ear tuned to the wind.

You can't ignore the surge and burst of a winter storm. There is a strange quality to the pitch of the wind—not the rebel yell of an ocean gale, but rather like the firm tone of a high executioner who takes off his coat, dons his mask, whets his axe, and says, "Bend your head."

A winter wind means business. It shakes "the walls as though a giant's hand were on them," and its wail is not like the childlike sighs of summer but the bellow of an angry curmudgeon.

However, winter stirs a challenge in man. When the storm was at its peak, I wanted to bundle up, race outdoors, and pitch myself against the pelting snow. As the whirlpools of snow swirled, I felt a gradual temper rising in me to get out there and fight.

Fight with what? My fists? A snow shovel would have been better, except I'm not supposed to wield one.

Anyway, a winter storm excites and dares you to brave its elements. It doesn't soothe and lull you with summer's sweet aromas and breathy lullabies. It's like a street-corner bully who yells, "Comeonout and put up yer dukes . . . or I'll come in afterya."

I'm old enough now to resist the challenge, after a brief wrestle with my adventurous soul.

The kids took up the battle. They dashed outside with their dogs, hurled themselves into snow drifts, let the wind toss them whirling, whirling, whirling, and then they and the dogs struggled against the snow, their voices defiantly piercing the wailing wind.

When the children returned to the house with red

noses and bright eyes, I felt a little guilty, like an old soldier who can no longer go off to the wars.

I think I know now why I don't like winter. The old bully has thrown me a challenge . . . and all I do is throw another log on the fire and raise my voice a little louder to fend off his bitter summons.

All I can do is watch my children accept his invitation.

—ross

I DON'T know how the rest of you reacted to the recent two feet of snow, but after it had fallen, and after some kindly people dug the Lehmans out of it, and after the sky cleared to sun and to the meticulous stars, that is to say, after the ball was over, I wandered out in the aftermath and found that great splendor had come to the earth.

I wanted to catch the splendor in its newness and freshness, before it grew stale or trampled or gray. Cars looked better under the white covering from the skies. One of them sailed jauntily by with a pillbox hat of snow perched on its roof, and I thought how its hat would melt as fast as fashions change.

All the trees, ordinarily so brittle and forbidding against a winter sky, were gently but forcibly outlined. Every place upon them that wasn't vertical, every slanting twig that bent toward a branch, every branch that blended toward the trunk, was quietly laden and sharply noticeable. And then sudden little winds whipped through them, sending the snow flying and making the trees look as if they were impatiently shaking themselves like wet shaggy dogs.

The colorful hats of tiny children moved headlessly between the banks of shoveled walks, reminding me of all the big people who have forgotten how it was when they were little and insist that we don't have the big snows that we used to have.

Children are close to the soil and the sky and are easily impressed. My smallest daughter made leg prints through the snow, expecting my four-year-old boy to follow her. The little boy was shoulder-high in her prints and completely out of his element. I watched him struggle for, oh, I'd say less than a minute before I rescued him, even though I knew that my minute was his long hour.

I walked at night between the snowbanks, knowing that this particular snow would be a long time turning gray, and longing for the secret of taking your time about melting and turning gray.

I felt wrapped in clean whiteness as I walked, and all the sounds I heard dropped clear as stars into my ears: voices, car horns, footsteps, motors. When I walked back to my own house, I saw that all the windows were blinking under the snowcapped roof, and overhead, nearly touching the rooftop, was a star that put all my tears to shame.

—**katey**

I saw a lonely star last night.

I stood on the porch and glanced at the star through a network of pine, and a film of clouds danced around it. There in the black sky it shone, almost lost in the vastness.

I was lonely, too. Oh, it wasn't a family misunderstanding or an unfulfilled longing. Only, at that moment, I felt hung in space, surrounded by many other stars . . . but billions of miles away from them.

There were no words in me to go inside the house then and explain my loneliness. How could I say that billions of years opened to me suddenly, billions of people flowed through me from the beginning of time, and I felt like a grain of sand tossed by capricious, heedless waves.

The awfulness of time, where there is no genesis or ending, no counting in the cosmic order or disorder, hit me. Yet time, as we little humans measure it, limits me to a snap of a finger—my lifetime—in the countless eons before me and after me.

My mind cried out, ached with the want to comprehend my place here, to know why my thought was winging to the star and back to the small light of my consciousness, and sought the core of what I am, why I am, and who I am.

This is my enigma, I said to the cold wind. I am living. I breathe the fragrant blossoms of spring, I love the blue eyes of my Katey, I touch the sturdy shoulder of my son, I see the golden hair of my daughter, I pursue the cool thoughts of Emerson, I revel like a drunken sailor on his first leave at all the essences of life around me . . . and I must lose it. I am a mortal. I am full of friends, full of love, full of the earth . . . and I must lose it.

I am fifty years of age, I told myself, and I have not learned that "there is a time to be born and a time to die." There is the rub. I'm so fascinated by this earth that I haven't learned how to leave it.

Suddenly, I shuddered. "Star bright," I said, "there is one advantage I have over you. I can move toward light and warmth."

I opened the door and came into the living room. There my wife looked up from the book she was reading and smiled . . . and her smile was an eternity.

"Thank God," I said to myself, "for my mind, which can perceive the light behind a smile; for my eyes, which can take in the beauty of a single dew-touched rose; for my hands, which can shape a word beyond a word; and for my voice, which can sing a lilting melody."

The loneliness is still there, will always be there, but there is a deep comfort here, too. As long as a person can touch another with his soul, he can live a billion years in his short lifetime.

—ross

Epilogue

ALL I know is that I am here.

And that is all I know, except for the silent thought that I shall not be here, as I am, forever.

I love lichen. From my first moments of awareness, I have loved lichen. When I walked through the woods, I looked down at where I was walking, and here and there, always near the stones and moss where my feet fell, I saw the tiny red lichen.

As a growing thing, before and after adolescence, I caught sight of lichen, and I was moved by it, and I was moved by the stones around it, and often, in a secret hollow of my mind, I wanted to bend and embrace the earth that had made the stones and moss and lichen.

Somewhere near the lichen and the stones and moss, there was water rippling, and it came to my ears out of its ancientness. I heard it well, and it was singing through the centuries of life.

Somehow the lichen came into me and gave me love and children. The earth made me and the lichen, and out of the earth, with its stones and waters, my children came into being.

I shall grow old, as all live things grow old, as I have watched tender crickets chirp their last sounds, as I have watched leaves part silently from their branches, as I have watched snow cover, and cover, and cover again.

I am here now, at this moment, and that is all I know. But loving lichen so, I shall somehow conduct myself properly and lovingly, so that in future times, when I have reluctantly given way to the silent secrets of the earth and have become part of them, unaware, the lichen will come again to someone who can bend his heart to see it.

—**katey**